involved IN Poetry

denise scott
david kitchen

HEINEMANN
EDUCATIONAL

Heinemann Educational Books Ltd
Halley Court, Jordan Hill, Oxford OX2 8EJ

OXFORD LONDON EDINBURGH
MELBOURNE SYDNEY AUCKLAND
IBADAN NAIROBI GABARONE HARARE
KINGSTON PORTSMOUTH NH (USA)
SINGAPORE MADRID

© Denise Scott 1987
adaptations © David Kitchen 1989
First published 1987 by Heinemann Educational Australia
This edition, adapted by David Kitchen, first published by Heinemann
Educational Books Ltd 1989

ISBN 0 435 14040 X

Cover Design by Design Revolution
Illustration by Sue Field

Designed by Lynda Patullo
Edited by Janet Blagg
Typeset in Bembo by Bookset, Melbourne
Adaptations typeset in Great Britain by Tradespools Ltd
Printed in Great Britain by Butler & Tanner Ltd, Frome and London

Contents

Introduction

When I was asked to consider preparing an edition of 'Involved in Poetry' the first thing that struck me was how different it was to the approach of many books, especially those that cover the years of public examinations.

Here was a writer who enthused about poetry where others treated it in terms of dutiful dissection. In addition, here was a book that encouraged groups to talk about poetry in a variety of specific and challenging contexts.

The book is likely to serve at least two important purposes. Firstly, it provides more than enough material to form the basis of a complete poetry course leading to GCSE or Standard grade examinations. Secondly it provides an alternative that can be used to supplement and add variety to existing material.

With more able groups, I believe it would also make a stimulating poetry course in the year prior to the start of public examinations.

In Part I, 'Listening and speaking', most of the basic elements of poetry are explored through discussions and games. Many of the activities are in the form of structured group discussions, in which positive group roles are introduced along with other techniques to develop

the skills in communication and the sharing of ideas so vital to language development.

Part II, 'Reading and writing', provides more in-depth explorations, beginning with extended reading. There is a chapter on reading poetry aloud: the vocal presentation of poems from simple readings to group productions. The final two chapters present activities to inspire and stimulate students in the creation of their own poetry.

One of the book's great advantages is that within its pages you will find almost all you need. There is no teacher's book to be balanced precariously alongside everything else on the desk and to be lost before crucial lessons. The one item missing from the book is the one item that it can never provide: the teacher's own interest and enthusiasm.

When that is added to what is already between these covers, I think you will have a powerful means of achieving a target that all too often seems unreasonably difficult: that of getting young people involved in poetry.

DAVID KITCHEN

1
Listening and speaking

1

Discussion in pairs

*S*haring thoughts and ideas is an important aspect of learning and of developing language skills. Often, it is not until we begin to explore and 'toss around' thoughts and ideas in language that they actually become clear to us. Further, we can only test and enrich our own responses by sharing and comparing them with others.

Instant reactions

1 Write a brief 'instant reaction' paper of at least six lines in response to each (one at a time) of the following six poems. Your reactions should be purely personal, with no preceding discussion with your partner.

2 Now exchange papers and write comments on each other's efforts.

3 As a pair, discuss each poem and try to decide on a suitable title.

4 If the whole class has been working on the activity, share the results of your discussions, then check page 145 to find the poems' real titles.

1
ACTIVITY

Retired a year now, Bert makes
a bitter joke about his cancer,
just discovered but far-gone.

"Gotta have something to do
when you're retired. This way,
at least I won't die of boredom."

And he leaves it at that, shunning
any but the barest of outlines
as worthless. "Only politicians

talk, and a lot of good that does."
A minute later, he includes
managers and radio-announcers

in his considered list of scourges.
He takes his tea carefully, with
its permitted bland foods, and then

leaves the table for ten minutes
in the tiled and sterile bathroom,
where he can deal with his fate's biology.

. . .

Beryl tells us that his late evening habit
is to sit hunched on the front steps before bed,
searching in the stars for further ways to cope.

ROSS CLARK

I heard them say I'm ugly.
I hoped it wasn't true.
I looked into the mirror
To get a better view,
And certainly my face seemed
Uninteresting and sad
I *wish* that either it was good
Or else just very bad.

My eyes are green, my hair is straight,
My ears stick out, my nose
Has freckles on it all the year,
I'm skinny as a hose.
If only I could look as I
Imagine I might be.
Oh, all the crowds would turn and bow,
They don't – because I'm me.

ELIZABETH JENNINGS

In the east
the sea is expected to run
silver the hour between four and five.
In the west, darkness may brood
a while longer.
Stars are predicted, but will clear
soon after dawn.

Masses of air will glide
from one place to another throughout the day.
Following dawn, the green tops of trees
will be subject to motion.
Under this condition, leaves are inclined
to clot the grass underfoot.

Throughout the day also
light and shade will alternate.
Dappled effects may follow,
elsewhere sharp divisions will be noted
especially between stands of trees
and open ground.

At six in the evening, the darkness
previously observed in the west
will build up in the east.
This will occur more forcefully
in the north than the south.
In the south a scattering of stars
is expected to pursue the sun slowly,
while the north will face a condition
of abrupt darkness, modified by the same stars
arriving earlier, and in greater numbers.

At four or five in the morning
a pale instability is predicted,
influencing the light of the stars
and the colour of the sea, which as previously noted
turns silver at this early hour.

ROGER McDONALD

I heard a thousand blended notes,
While in a grove I sate reclined,
In that sweet mood when pleasant thoughts
Bring sad thoughts to the mind.

To her fair works did Nature link
The human soul that through me ran;
And much it grieved my heart to think
What man has made of man.

Through primrose tufts, in that green bower,
The periwinkle trailed its wreaths;
And 'tis my faith that every flower
Enjoys the air it breathes.

The birds around me hopped and played,
Their thoughts I cannot measure:—
But the least motion which they made,
It seemed a thrill of pleasure.

The budding twigs spread out their fan,
To catch the breezy air;
And I must think, do all I can,
That there was pleasure there.

If this belief from heaven be sent,
If such be Nature's holy plan,
Have I not reason to lament
What man has made of man?

WILLIAM WORDSWORTH

My mistress' eyes are nothing like the sun;
Coral is far more red than her lips' red;
If snow be white, why then her breasts are dun;
If hairs be wires, black wires grow on her head.
I have seen roses damask'd, red, and white,
But no such roses see I in her cheeks;
And in some perfumes is there more delight
Than in the breath that from my mistress reeks.
I love to hear her speak; yet well I know
That music hath a far more pleasing sound.
I grant I never saw a goddess go;
My mistress, when she walks, treads on the ground.
And yet, by heaven, I think my love as rare
As any she beli'd with false compare.

WILLIAM SHAKESPEARE

I remember
last July
in Jindabyne,
when I saw
him,
with another
girl,
in
Maxims.
I stood,
in the
lightly falling
snow,
and watched
him,
through a
big window.
He was
hand in hand
with her.
I felt
my heart beat
so fast,
and my hands,
came down
empty.

ELIZABETH MITCHELL
(STUDENT)

Comprehension

Read the following poem individually, then with your partner discuss
the statements which follow it. Together, decide whether you agree,
disagree with, or are unsure of your stand on, each statement.

The Hunchback in the Park

The hunchback in the park
A solitary mister
Propped between trees and water
From the opening of the garden lock
That lets the trees and water enter
Until the Sunday sombre bell at dark

Eating bread from a newspaper
Drinking water from the chained cup
That the children filled with gravel
In the fountain basin where I sailed my ship
Slept at night in a dog kennel
But nobody chained him up.

Like the park birds he came early
Like the water he sat down
And Mister they called Hey mister
The truant boys from the town
Running when he had heard them clearly
On out of sound

Past lake and rockery
Laughing when he shook his paper
Hunchbacked in mockery
Through the loud zoo of the willow groves
Dodging the park keeper
With his stick that picked up leaves.

And the old dog sleeper
Alone between nurses and swans
While the boys among willows
Made the tigers jump out of their eyes
To roar on the rockery stones
And the groves were blue with sailors

Made all day until bell time
A woman figure without fault
Straight as a young elm
Straight and tall from his crooked bones
That she might stand in the night
After the locks and chains

DYLAN THOMAS

Statements about *Hunchback in the Park*

1 The hunchback is compared to a dog.

2 The poem's theme is our inhumanity to each other—especially those different or less fortunate.

3 The poem's theme is children's innocent ability to hurt and mock others.

4 The animal-related imagery in the poem is meant to imply that people, in their desperation, will assume animal instincts and actions.

5 While seemingly very much like prose, 'Hunchback' is full of subtle, poetic rhyme, eg internal rhyme: 'With his stick that picked up leaves'; assonance and alliteration. (Assonance and alliteration are explained on page 57.)

6 The poem's flowing, unpunctuated movement suggests the monotony and continuity of the old man's life in the park.

7 The poem has no definite mood or feeling so it is difficult to assess Thomas' attitude to the boys and the old man.

Exploring imagery

In the following activity we feature the work of Emma Payne, a student who won a major award in a national poetry competition. Her particular poetic skill lies in the use of imagery.

NOTES

Poets may use aural, visual or tactile images to appeal to our senses.
- **Aural images:** these help us to *hear* the sounds the poet is describing, for example: 'the stuttering rifle's rapid rattle'.
- **Tactile images:** through these we can better appreciate the *touch* or the *feeling* of what the poet is describing, for example: 'the breeze, chill-fingered, needle sharp'.
- **Visual images:** by far the most common, these help us to *see* what the poet is describing, for example: 'the children, flower-scattered at their play'.

While these images may simply be single words or phrases, poets may also use special devices of imagery—similes, metaphors and personification—to help us experience a situation more vividly.

Simile

A simile is a direct, stated comparison; the poet writes that something is *like* or *as* something else, for example: 'as clean as cold', 'like blowflies my eyes would crawl'.

Metaphor

A poet uses metaphor when speaking of people or objects as though they were something else. This substitution (also a form of comparison) helps illustrate an attribute or feature of the object or person in question, for example: 'a waterfall of grass', 'a pane of sky', 'her glacial eyes'.

Personification

When a poet speaks of an inanimate object as though it were a person, he or she is using personification, for example: 'the morning comes to consciousness', 'the winter evening settles down'.

Read the following poems by Emma Payne and in pairs discuss them. The following questions may help you in your discussion.
- Does she show a preference for any particular type of imagery?
- Do the poems show any other poetic skills?
- Did you think, at any time, that the imagery was too obvious?
- Which poem, in your opinion, is most effective and why is it?

**3
ACTIVITY**

Write down your findings, which one member of the pair will report to the whole class, being careful not to repeat points or examples made by previous speakers.

Yorkshire

Flint walls cuts
the puckered land,
Crag houses have splintered and thrust up
out of the dark earth,
they squat uneasily on the hillsides

A countryside of bog and moor,
mist and drizzle,
Its people rise up
out of ditches
and its slow heart beats
in the roots of the damp heather

The Boxer

The great iron figure crouches,
Scabs like flowers on his knees,
And his chest is like a mountain
And his legs are thick as trees.

He spits blood like a cherub
In a fountain spouting foam,
Ringed around by swinging ropes
And punters going home.

Broken-knuckled, shiny-eyed,
Battered, bruised, and wet
With droplets like cold rubies,
And laced with bitter sweat.

He crouches in a corner
In his pool of sparkling red
And dreads the jeers which soon will fall
Like blows upon his head.

Early Swim

The night cracks,
and dawn
spills out on the water

The river bubbles;
A white limb flashes somewhere,
down in the darkness,
it sinks like a stone,
and silence hangs, like death,
over the black water

As brown reeds tangle
with blond hair,
a flower bends
and drops its heavy petals
over the surface;
white eyes stare out of the depths

Suddenly the surface explodes
into droplets; lungs
gasp for air,
and pale arms grab for the bank

A bird in the weeping willow
bursts into wild song

Dockland

In the man is the boy
Who thundered on short legs,
Snorting and sniffing,
Down to Dockland

To banging, rattling land's edge.
Peopled by men with muscles like great chains
Binding their arms, and voices like hammers;
To splinters and sawdust and rotten fruit
Oozing brown; to brutal cobbles and broken crates
And slated, gaping windows, and brawls and shouting
In the shipyards, howling saws and curling wood,
And the black, stinking puddles of sea water
Which rotted the iron anchors

Among tall ships and screaming birds the seed was sown:
As he sits, pinstriped, at his desk, eyes on the clock,
His longing unfolds inside him like a huge sail.
Mentally he runs up a wooden gangplank
Onto a departing ship.

Aural imagery

Mental pictures or 'images' are fundamental to nearly all kinds of writing. Nearly everything we read creates a picture in our mind, consciously or subconsciously. Poets, being creative writers, are particularly aware of the power of the mental image or impact created by carefully chosen words and phrases.

Just as words can conjure up visual images, they can also conjure aural images—impressions of various sound sensations. Aural imagery can be created in two main ways.

Onomatopoeia

Onomatopoeia is the use of words which directly imitate sounds, for example: whoosh, boom, tick tock, spit, mumble. What others can you think of?

The Rime of the Ancient Mariner by Samuel Taylor Coleridge has many examples of aural imagery created by onomatopoeia:

> The ice was here, the ice was there,
> The ice was all around:
> It cracked and growled, and roared and howled,
> Like noises in a swound!

Sound pictures

A poet can also create pictures in the mind which help us to hear the sound or sounds. Again, from The Rime of the Ancient Mariner:

> Down dropt the breeze, the sails dropt down,
> 'Twas sad as sad could be;
> And we did speak only to break
> The silence of the sea!

With the mood of calm and despair created by the first two lines, it is easy to 'hear' the silence punctuated by the rarely spoken word.

4
ACTIVITY

You could, if you like, obtain a copy of The Rime of the Ancient Mariner and look at the use of aural imagery in the entire poem. It makes for exciting reading.

Meanwhile, in pairs, study the following poems and determine why each is an excellent example of the use of aural imagery. Again, one member of each pair will report back to the whole class.

Anthem for Doomed Youth

What passing-bells for these who die as cattle?
   Only the monstrous anger of the guns.
   Only the stuttering rifles' rapid rattle
Can patter out their hasty orisons.
No mockeries now for them; no prayers nor bells,
   Nor any voice of mourning save the choirs,—
The shrill, demented choirs of wailing shells;
   And bugles calling for them from sad shires.

What candles may be held to speed them all?
   Not in the hands of boys, but in their eyes
Shall shine the holy glimmers of good-byes.
   The pallor of girls' brows shall be their pall;
Their flowers the tenderness of patient minds,
And each slow dusk a drawing-down of blinds.

WILFRED OWEN

The Night-Ride

Gas flaring on the yellow platform; voices running up and down;
Milk-tins in cold dented silver; half-awake I stare.
Pull up the blind, blink out—all sounds are drugged;
The slow blowing of passengers asleep;
Engines yawning; water in heavy drips;
Black, sinister travellers, lumbering up the station,
One moment in the window, hooked over bags;
Hurrying, unknown faces—boxes with strange labels—
All groping clumsily to mysterious ends,
Out of the gaslight, dragged by private Fates.
Their echoes die. The dark train shakes and plunges;
Bells cry out; the night-ride starts again.
Soon I shall look out into nothing but blackness,
Pale, windy fields. The old roar and knock of the rails
Melts in dull fury. Pull down the blind. Sleep. Sleep.
Nothing but grey, rushing rivers of bush outside.
Gaslight and milk-cans. Of Rapptown I recall nothing else.

KENNETH SLESSOR

ACTIVITY

Close reading

Read this poem paying particular attention to the meaning of the imagery.

Then, through discussion with your partner, decide on how well the statements which follow the poem relate to it.

If called on during a class discussion, you must be prepared to explain the reasons for your decisions.

Dulce et Decorum Est

Bent double, like old beggars under sacks,
Knock-kneed, coughing like hags, we cursed through sludge,
Till on the haunting flares we turned our backs,
And towards our distant rest began to trudge.
Men marched asleep. Many had lost their boots,
But limped on, blood-shod. All went lame, all blind;
Drunk with fatigue; deaf even to the hoots
Of gas-shells dropping softly behind.

Gas! Gas! Quick, boys!—An ecstasy of fumbling,
Fitting the clumsy helmets just in time,
But someone still was yelling out and stumbling
And floundering like a man in fire or lime.—
Dim through the misty panes and thick green light,
As under a green sea, I saw him drowning.
In all my dreams, before my helpless sight,
He plunges at me, guttering, choking, drowning.

If in some smothering dreams, you too could pace
Behind the wagon that we flung him in,
And watch the white eyes writhing in his face,
His hanging face, like a devil's sick of sin;
If you could hear, at every jolt, the blood
Come gargling from the froth-corrupted lungs,
Obscene as cancer, bitter as the cud
Of vile, incurable sores on innocent tongues,—
My friend, you would not tell with such high zest
To children ardent for some desperate glory,
The old Lie: Dulce et decorum est
Pro patria mori.

WILFRED OWEN

Statements about *Dulce et Decorum Est*

Part 1: Which of these statements are actually *represented* in the poem? They may be expressed differently in the poem, but the meaning must be the same.

1 The soldiers are retreating because of injuries that have left them blind, deaf or lame.

2 The soldiers' feet are caked with blood.

3 The soldiers are tired from consuming too much alcohol.

4 The soldiers really enjoy the challenge of fitting their gas masks in time.

5 There is no pleasure in dying in war, even if it is for one's country.

6 It is the innocent who suffer and die in war.

7 War is never justified.

Part 2: Which of these statements, or attitudes, can be *deduced* from the general content of the poem?

1 Owen has not been hardened or desensitized by the suffering he has seen.

2 The glory of war can attract prospective army recruits.

3 War leaves mental as well as physical scars.

4 War creates pacifists.

5 Owen is revolted by the ugly and senseless sufferings of war.

6 Death through being gassed is slow, painful and pitiful.

7 Most people believe it is honourable to die for one's country in war.

2
Whole group discussions

*T*he discussions in this chapter are designed to involve everyone. And when everyone gives themselves fully to the creative and harmonious functioning of the group the activities can be not only productive but enjoyable as well.

Listening and responding—
'Your number's up'

ACTIVITY

Any of the following four poems should be suitable for this activity.

1 Each member of the group is given a number and the numbers are put in a hat.

2 The teacher, or a selected student, reads one of the following poems aloud, a few times if necessary.

3 A number is drawn and called. The class member with that number must respond spontaneously to the poem. There are no restrictions upon the comment except that it should be relevant and appropriate.

4 When the first person has finished speaking, a second number is drawn and that group member must speak. Ideally the new speaker should respond to the first speaker's comments (elaborating, contradicting, agreeing) rather than taking a new direction. If this is not possible, any appropriate comment will do.

5 This process continues until class comment on that poem seems to have been exhausted.

Sad Aunt Madge

As the cold winter evenings drew near
Aunt Madge used to put extra blankets
over the furniture, to keep it warm and cosy.
Mussolini was her lover, and life
was an outoffocus rosy-tinted spectacle.

but neurological experts
with kind blueeyes
and gentle voices
small white hands
and large Rolls Royces
said that electric shock treatment
should do the trick
it did . . .

today after 15 years of therapeutic tears
and an awful lot of ratepayers' shillings
down the hospital meter
sad Aunt Madge
no longer tucks up the furniture
before kissing it goodnight
and admits
that her affair with Mussolini
clearly was not right
particularly in the light
of her recently announced engagement
to the late pope.

ROGER McGOUGH

Song for Last Year's Wife

Alice, this is my first winter
of waking without you, of knowing
that you, dressed in familiar clothes
are elsewhere, perhaps not even
conscious of our anniversary. Have
you noticed? The earth's still as hard,
the same empty gardens exist; it is
as if nothing special had changed.

I wake with another mouth feeding
from me, yet still feel as if
Love had not the right
to walk out of me. A year now. So
what? you say. I send out my spies
to discover what you are doing. They smile,
return, tell me your body's as firm,
you are as alive, as warm and inviting
as when I knew you first . . . Perhaps it is
the winter, its isolation from other seasons,
that sends me your ghost to witness
when I wake. Somebody came here today, asked
how you were keeping, what
you were doing. I imagine you,
waking in another city, touched
by this same hour. So ordinary
a thing as loss comes now and touches me.

BRIAN PATTEN

Cows

Cows graze across the hill
Measuring the day
As their shadows tell
Irrelevant time. Their gait is half-way
Between moving and standing still.

The sun is gentle on the green
Of their meadow, their mouths deep
In its heavy warmth.
A watcher could fall asleep
Into the depth
Of that untroubled scene.

From each dewdrop morning
To every day's end
They follow the cycle
Of the rhythm of the world turning
In its season. A miracle
Of normalcy is a cow's mind.

Beyond thought's prickling fever
They dwell in the grace
Of their own true concerns.
And in that place
Know they will live forever
With butterflies around their horns.

PETER KOCAN

Mr Smith's Collection

I see you, taking it slowly,
The five dozen yards to the shop,
A brief hallo, a nod, no smile,
A long asthmatic stop.

You'd ask for half a cabbage,
Stare blankly straight ahead,
Choose two or three potatoes,
Buy yesterday's cheap bread.

I liked you Mr Smith.
That's something you wouldn't know.
I would smile but keep on playing,
Mum might say hello.

I never went inside your house,
Dusty, dark, smelling strange.
Time had let it stand apart,
Unmoved, unmarked by change.

You can't have relished life at all,
That last unchanging year,
Regular and solitary,
No friends or family near.

My mother told me you had "gone",
She made it sound quite planned.
I asked her to explain. She said
I wouldn't understand.

I understood what happened next:
They stripped your private corners,
Went through the house's secrets
Like vultures more than mourners.

They cannot harm you, Mr Smith,
That's the best of being "gone".
Did you ever know or guess though
What they would light upon?

The china, so my father says,
Is beautiful and rare.
I'm sorry that I never saw it
When you were living there.

I'm sorry, too, you kept it hid.
"A waste," my mother said.
A shame, too, when I think you bought
Yesterday's cheap bread.

If you were still alive, mind,
If only for a while,
I wouldn't want to just see plates
I'd want to see you smile.

DAVID KITCHEN

Dramatic analysis—'Teacher in role'

A well written dramatic monologue can be one of the most powerfully effective poetic forms. Such is the case with Robert Browning's *My Last Duchess*. A simple role play will help unravel the mystery (and initial difficulty) of this cleverly executed poem.

ACTIVITY

The teacher (or a selected student) should thoroughly acquaint herself or himself with Browning's poem, ready to give a convincing reading of it.

My Last Duchess

Ferrara

That's my last Duchess painted on the wall,
Looking as if she were alive. I call
That piece a wonder, now: Fra Pandolf's hands
Worked busily a day, and there she stands.
Will't please you sit and look at her? I said
'Fra Pandolf' by design, for never read
Strangers like you that pictured countenance,
The depth and passion of its earnest glance,
But to myself they turned (since none puts by
The curtain I have drawn for you, but I)
And seemed as they would ask me, if they durst,
How such a glance came there; so, not the first
Are you to turn and ask thus. Sir, 'twas not
Her husband's presence only, called that spot
Of joy into the Duchess' cheek: perhaps
Fra Pandolf chanced to say 'Her mantle laps
Over my lady's wrist too much,' or 'Paint
Must never hope to reproduce the faint
Half-flush that dies along her throat:' such stuff
Was courtesy, she thought, and cause enough
For calling up that spot of joy. She had
A heart—how shall I say?—too soon made glad,
Too easily impressed; she liked whate'er
She looked on, and her looks went everywhere.
Sir, 'twas all one! My favour at her breast,
The dropping of the daylight in the West,
The bough of cherries some officious fool
Broke in the orchard for her, the white mule
She rode with round the terrace—all and each
Would draw from her alike the approving speech,
Or blush, at least. She thanked men,—good! but thanked
Somehow—I know not how—as if she ranked
My gift of a nine-hundred-years-old name
With anybody's gift. Who'd stoop to blame
This sort of trifling? Even had you skill
In speech—(which I have not)—to make your will
Quite clear to such an one, and say, 'Just this
Or that in you disgusts me; here you miss,
Or there exceed the mark'—and if she let

Herself be lessoned so, nor plainly set
Her wits to yours, forsooth, and made excuse,
—E'en then would be some stooping; and I choose
Never to stoop. Oh sir, she smiled, no doubt,
Whene'er I passed her; but who passed without
Much the same smile? This grew; I gave commands;
Then all smiles stopped together. There she stands
As if alive. Will't please you rise? We'll meet
The company below, then. I repeat,
The Count your master's known munificence
Is ample warrant that no just pretence
Of mine for dowry will be disallowed;
Though his fair daughter's self, as I avowed
At starting, is my object. Nay, we'll go
Together down, sir. Notice Neptune, though,
Taming a sea-horse, thought a rarity,
Which Claus of Innsbruck cast in bronze for me!

ROBERT BROWNING

1 You, the class, are the Duke's 'visitor'—his monologue is addressed to you. Listen intently. The teacher takes on the role of the Duke and proceeds to read the poem to you, his visitor, being sure to adopt the Duke's detached tone and arrogant attitude.

   To add realism and impact, deliver the monologue from an elevated position and have a large portrait of a woman to refer to (details for such a portrait are in the poem)!

   Repeat this 'performance' if it is felt necessary.

2 Form pairs to prepare questions to ask the Duke. These questions should be designed to help you understand the Duke's situation, his motives, attitude, intentions and language.

3 In your role as the 'visitor' address your questions to the Duke, who will hopefully be able to provide the answers.

4 When you all feel you understand the situation described in the poem, roles can be dropped, and the following questions can be raised for discussion:

   a What is the Duke's present situation? Of what was his wife guilty?
   b Why has the Duke's visitor come?
   c Describe the Duke's character as fully as you can, using the 'evidence' from the poem.
   d What is the effect of the last three lines of the poem?
   e How appropriate is the title of the poem?
   f Comment on the tone of the poem. Would you say it is the poem's outstanding feature?
   g We call this poem a 'dramatic monologue'. Think about the meaning of each of these words. Why do you think *My Last Duchess* is a dramatic monologue? (For an explanation of this as a poetic form, see page 72.)

3

ACTIVITY

You can use the teacher-in-role technique with any dramatic monologue. Try it with this contemporary poem.

Emporium

Young Lady, what can I do for you?
Yes, of course, you want a lover.
We have this unrepeatable offer:
this beautiful model with floating hair.
Just look at the eyes! Of course it's tricky
to handle, the only one of its kind.
Think how your friends will envy you.

My dear young lady, back already?
So the model got out of control in the dark?
And the words he used when he chose to speak
didn't seem to suit your lovely home?
And your parents insist on trading him in?

Well, may I suggest our regular number,
our knitting-book type, as cool and smooth
as his cigarette, in Alpine drag,
germ-free complete with sag-proof smile.

Good morning, Madam, yes I can guess,
you've settled down and you'd like a child.
They come in all kinds, you can take your pick.
This one won't give you a moment's worry:
all-girl, all-boy, yes, one of each,
good on their potties, pretty and clean,
obedient socially well-adjusted.
What else could Madam possibly want?

Good morning, good morning, of course I remember.
If Madam was so dissatisfied
why did she not say so at the time?
Diseases, nightmares, obscure neuroses?—
Dear lady, those models were factory-clean
and we couldn't possibly trade them in.

But down in the basement we happen to have
that very old model with flashing eyes
(and hair still good!) . . . If Madam cares
to take it away she might possibly find
a part that could be used to fill
that gaping hole in Madam's heart.

T. F. KLINE

Fish-bowl discussion

Goals

- To involve the whole class in a discussion, either as participants or observers, in a co-operative group climate where everyone is encouraged to assume and develop 'leadership skills'.
- To develop skills in exploring poetry; supporting your opinions and assessing the opinions of others.
- To develop skills in observing and giving constructive feedback on the processes of discussion and decision-making.

Group organisation

The class is divided into three groups: *participants* (half the class), *process observers* and *content observers* (each one quarter of the class). These roles are rotated for each new activity.

Seating arrangement

You can see from the diagram why this is called a 'fish-bowl' discussion.

- The **participants** (group A) form a circle, facing each other.
- The **process observers** (group B) form an outer circle, so that they can focus on two participants opposite them.
- The **content observers** (group C) sit outside the circle, elevated on desks or tables so as to be able to clearly see and hear the whole proceedings.

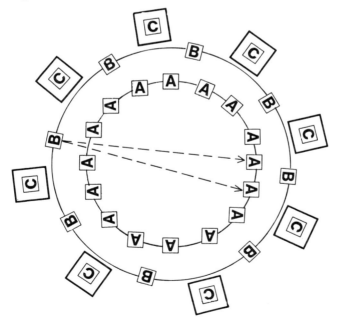

Group tasks

- **Group A** participates in the discussion.
- **Group B** members closely observe and note the discussion techniques of the two participants sitting opposite them. For this purpose a checklist is provided, a copy of which should be made for each observer for each activity. See page 25.
- **Group C** members note the content of the discussion, drawing together the points made into a summary, or synthesis, to present to the whole class at the end of the discussion. Their reports can be delivered orally, in writing, or they can confer together to present one main synthesis.

Process observers' feedback (Group B)

The whole purpose of this process observation is to make us aware of our group 'style' so that, ultimately, we can improve it. We can do this by knowing what positive group roles make the group more cohesive and productive. A knowledge of negative group roles should also make us more self-critical and aware of the effects of negative behaviour on group effectiveness.

After the process observers have given their feedback, participants can consider the following questions:

- Did you feel you were correctly assessed by your observer?
- Do you feel that you usually play the sort of role the observer assessed you as playing?
- If you weren't cited in the positive feedback, does it mean you were playing a negative role? Is silence necessarily a negative role?
- Do you think you could perform in any of the other roles in the interests of group effectiveness?

Process observer checklist

Positive group roles		
1 Participates in the discussion		
2 Contributes 'evidence' or relevant information		
3 Asks questions or opinions of others		
4 Listens attentively to others		
5 Initiates action or direction		
6 Trys to keep the group lively		
7 Trys to keep the discussion moving		
8 Encourages contribution of others		
9 Clarifies an issue		
10 Helps resolve misunderstanding or conflict		

Negative group roles
Note: All the attributes listed here are positive ones. Be aware, too, of negative contributions or roles. These include:

- Being too dominant or aggressive
- Showing apathy or indifference
- Competing or clashing with others
- Frequently straying from the topic
- Engaging in distracting or disruptive behaviour

Fish-bowl 1: Poetic purpose

4
ACTIVITY

1 Divide the class into participants, process observers and content observers as previously explained. In this exercise each process observer observes the *whole* group's interactions, and in the blanks provided on the checklist (page 25) enters the names of two group members who interacted most noticeably as indicated.

2 While everyone individually comes to an initial understanding of the following three poems, the process observers also take a little time to become familiar with the checklist.

Tourist Promotion

For the tourists, who stay in the
Large new tourist hotels, the
Chief tourist attractions are the
Other large new tourist hotels.

For the querulous and wayward
There were once the local monkeys,
Who lived in the ancient tree-tops
Long before the hotels were thought of.
The tourists enticed the monkeys down
From the trees with monkey nuts and
Breakfast rolls. And the monkeys
Scampered across the road and were
Squashed by the buses transporting
Fresh tourists to see the monkeys.
It was not a pretty sight.

So now the tourists are confined to
The tourist hotels, large and new.
They pass with the greatest of ease
From one to the other, escorted by porters
With large new umbrellas, or even through
Underground passages, air-conditioned and
Adorned with murals by local artists,
Conveying impressions of the local scene.
After all, the tourist hotels were created
Specifically for the sake of the tourists.

D.J. ENRIGHT

Much madness is divinest sense
To a discerning eye—
Much sense the starkest madness.
'Tis the majority
In this, as all, prevail.
Assent and you are sane;
Demur, you're straightway dangerous
And handled with a chain.

EMILY DICKINSON

The Examination

you set the first question
            you said
how much are you involved
            with me?
            and I
not being very good
            at maths
said I didn't know.
I set the second question
            I said
how do you measure
            an emotion?
            and you
not being very good
            at english
        smiled at me.

STEVE TURNER

3 The whole group makes the fish-bowl configuration described on page 23. The content observers take notes and the process observers make their group assessment while the participants discuss the following:

Assuming that any piece of literature worthy of the name has something worth while to say and says it in an artful, original or beautiful way, discuss the following questions with reference to the three poems.

a What is the chief purpose of each of these poems?
b Is the purpose worth while? How useful, fresh or original are the sentiments, facts or observations being expressed?
c How is the purpose achieved? That is, what aspects of form, style, imagery, language or other characteristics make the poem artful, beautiful or otherwise?

4 At the end of the discussion, process observers discuss their observations, and content observers give their reports (in any of the ways outlined on page 24, at the discretion of the teacher).

Fish-bowl 2: Poetry or not?

1 This activity will be similar to the previous one except that the class will divide into smaller groups.

But first, everyone, as individuals, take time to read and evaluate this group of poems. According to your personal definition of poetry—the criteria by which *you* decide what is or is not poetic—decide which of these pieces you consider worthy of the name 'poetry'.

Against or For Beauty

Peasant women etc
ox paddyfield & so on
plough slush straw hat
child in arms etc etc

delete arms insert on back
child on back—rub out
back insert backwards
child strapped on backwards

Peasant woman etc
screech run fall & so on
bullets napalm shrapnel
child in mud etc etc

delete mud insert broken
child broken—rub out
broken insert blown apart
child mangled blown apart

Peasant woman etc
what can we do & so on
being sickened is a luxury
aesthetics of pain etc etc

delete pain insert revolution
aesthetics of revolution—rub out
aesthetics insert beauty
revolution must be

RICHARD TIPPING

City Cafeteria

But one man compels notice:
Seventy-ish and dignified.
Picking absently at his food
In a meek confusion.
No gay city adventurer.
That suit, that snowy collar.
The shined shoes, are, to his era,
Garb for deaths and lawyers.

Reading him, one pictures
An old wife recently gone
And today the formal duties
of Wills and cold arrangements.
And again one feels the dark
Huge beneath the surface
Of things, that now has found the gap
Grief opens in one old man.

PETER KOCAN

To a Friend Under Sentence of Death

In about a week, they say
you will be gone.
It is valuable time.
I walk slowly about this town.
The heartbeat seems to have shifted somewhat
to dead centre under the breastbone
swinging the weight of a clock.
Displacements are unnatural.
So is the total disappearance of my car.
With perfect naturalness I walk about
making no inquiries, simply
pursuing whereabouts
in the grid of streets and meeting
with perfect naturalness Walter Mitty
round every next corner, hailing him gaily
for coffee, a cigarette, and what
in God's name to talk about,
to walk about, walk off
the map, to be better off without,
inwardly shaking, knowing you still
lying in this town. In about a week
they say blandly
who are not acquainted with death
on a week's rope
weight of a clock . . .

ANNE ELDER

If Jesus Was Born Today

If Jesus was born today
it would be in a downtown motel
marked by a helicopter's flashing bulb.
A traffic warden, working late,
would be the first upon the scene.
Later, at the expense of a TV network,
an eminent sociologist,
the host of a chat show
and a controversial author
would arrive with their good wishes
—the whole occasion to be filmed as part of the
'Is This The Son Of God?' one hour special.
Childhood would be a blur of photographs
and speculation
dwindling by His late teens into
'Where Is He Now?' features in Sunday magazines.

If Jesus was thirty today
they wouldn't really care about the public ministry,
they'd be too busy investigating His finances
and trying to prove He had Church or Mafia
connections.
The miracles would be explained by
an eminent and controversial magician,
His claims to be God's Son recognised as
excellent examples of Spoken English
and immediately incorporated into
the O-Level syllabus,
His sinless perfection considered by moral philosophers
as, OK, but a bit repressive.

If Jesus was thirty-one today
He'd be the fly in everyone's ointment—
the sort of controversial person who
stands no chance of eminence.
Communists would expel Him, capitalists
would exploit Him or have Him
smeared by people who know a thing or two about God.
Doctors would accuse Him of quackery,
soldiers would accuse Him of cowardice,
theologians would take Him aside and try
to persuade Him of His non-existence.

If Jesus was thirty-two today we'd have to
end it all. Heretic, fundamentalist, literalist,
puritan, pacifist, non-comformist, we'd take Him
away and quietly end the argument.
But the argument would rumble in the ground
at the end of three days and would break out
and walk around as though death was some bug
saying 'I am the resurrection and the life . . .
No man cometh to the Father but by me'.

While the magicians researched new explanations
and the semanticists wondered exactly what
He meant by 'I' and 'No man' there would be those
who stand around amused, asking for something
called proof.

STEVE TURNER

2 The class will now need to divide into smaller groups. Each group should have one process observer, one content observer and four, five or six participants.

3 Begin the discussion drawing on the poems you have just read. The topic: 'Poetry or not?'.

4 The process observers should attempt to deduce and assess the contribution made by the particular participants they are observing. In what way are they contributing to the efficient and harmonious functioning of the group?

5 At the end of the discussion, the observers make their reports to the whole group.

Fish-bowl 3: Analysis

6
ACTIVITY

1 On your own, read and explore the poem *Beach Burial*.

Beach Burial

Softly and humbly to the Gulf of Arabs
The convoys of dead sailors come;
At night they sway and wander in the waters far under,
But morning rolls them in the foam.

Between the sob and clubbing of the gunfire
Someone, it seems, has time for this,
To pluck them from the shallows and bury them in burrows
And tread the sand upon their nakedness;

And each cross, the driven stake of tidewood,
Bears the last signature of men,
Written with such perplexity, with such bewildered pity,
The words choke as they begin—

'*Unknown seaman*'—the ghostly pencil
Wavers and fades, the purple drips,
The breath of the wet season has washed their inscriptions
As blue as drowned men's lips,

Dead seamen, gone in search of the same landfall,
Whether as enemies they fought,
Or fought with us, or neither; the sand joins them together,
Enlisted on the other front.

El Alamein.

KENNETH SLESSOR

2 Still on your own, complete the following four statements.
  a I think this poem is about . . . . .
  b I think the best lines/phrases are . . . . . because . . . . .
  c I think Kenneth Slessor wrote the poem because . . . . .
  d I think the weakest thing about the poem is . . . . .

3 Divide into participants, content and process observers, and arrange the class as explained on page 23.

4 The discussion should be based on the four statements that have been produced by each member of the group. It is the job of the group to reach agreement about those four statements. Unanimous agreement is unlikely but that should be the aim.

5 While the discussion is running, the process observers follow the instructions on page 24. On a copy of the checklist, use one of the blank columns for each of the participants you are observing: put a mark in their column each time they interact noticeably as indicated. At the end, evaluate their contribution in each area on the basis of how many marks they received.

6 At the end of the discussion, content observers deliver their summaries and the process observers report (tactfully) on the strong and weak points of the two participants they were observing.

7 Take some time for discussion on the feedback. Is such feedback helping to improve the effectiveness of the group?

3
Consensus discussions

*T*he discussions in this chapter are structured as consensus-seeking activities. It is an attempt to reach agreement on an issue by allowing all parties in a dispute to state their position, listen to the arguments of others and alter (or retain) their views accordingly.

Guidelines for consensus

In these activities our aim is to reach consensus on the ranking (in order of validity) of certain statements about the poems under discussion.

Total agreement, or unanimity, is not necessarily the aim; this is rarely achieved. One's personal goal is to state—and support—one's own attitudes and opinions and to open-mindedly consider the logic and validity of others' views.

a Avoid *arguing* for your own rankings. Present your position as lucidly and logically as possible, but consider other members' reactions carefully before you press your point.

b Do not assume that someone must win and someone must lose when discussion reaches a stalemate. Instead, look for the next most acceptable alternative for all parties.

c Do not change your mind simply to avoid conflict. And when agreement comes quickly and easily, be suspicious. Explore the reasons and be sure everyone accepts the solution for basically similar, or

35

complementary, reasons. Yield only to positions that have objective and logically sound foundations.

d Avoid conflict reducing techniques such as majority vote, averages, coin-flips or bargaining. When a dissenting member finally agrees, don't feel that person must be rewarded by having his or her own way on some later point.

e Differences of opinion are natural and expected. Seek them out and try to involve everyone in the decision making process. Disagreements can help the group's decision because, with a wide range of input and opinions, there is a greater chance that the group will hit upon more adequate solutions.

f The actual wording of statements should be closely examined. Generalisations, for example: 'Teenagers wouldn't know any better', can usually be accorded a low rank. Watch for words like all, any, no, never; they often signal an overstatement, exaggeration, or generalisation.

g If you consider certain statements to be equally true, assign them the same ranking.

h If, after reasonable time and deliberation, consensus does not seem likely, make a general assessment of progress and close the discussion.

Procedure

1 Individually read and come to a general understanding of the poem.

2 Individually, rank the statements following each poem. If there are five statements, the statement you consider to be most true rank as 1, the statement you consider least true as 5, and rank the other statements 2, 3 and 4 accordingly. If there are nine statements, the least true would be ranked 9, etc.

   You will need at least ten minutes for this stage.

3 Now form groups of about eight. Six students take part in the discussion, while the other two observe.

4 One of the observers is to report on the group's performance, based on points a to f of the guidelines above. Alternatively, the report could be based on the 'Decision making styles' guide opposite. You will probably find that the style, or degree, of reaching consensus varies for each ranking decided.

5 The second observer is to prepare a brief appreciation of the poem from a summary of the group's deliberations.

6 Now, in your groups, attempt to reach consensus on the ranking of the statements. Use the same scale that you used in your individual ranking.

Decision making styles

Match the ranking of each statement with the style that was used to reach consensus.

1 **Complete consensus** Every member expresses support for the group's decision.

2 **Near consensus** One or two members may have doubts about the group's decision, but still agree to go along with it.

3 **Majority action** A majority supports the decision, over the minority's objections or silence.

4 **Minority action** Fewer than half of the group members support the decision.

5 **Unilateral action** One person initiates and carries through the decision, while the remaining members comply silently.

Statement   Rank   Style   Comments

1

2

3

4

5

6

7

8

9

1
ACTIVITY

Form and theme
Follow the guidelines for consensus on the preceding pages.

Standardization

When, darkly brooding on this Modern Age,
the journalist with his marketable woes
fills up once more the inevitable page
of fatuous, flatulent, Sunday-paper prose:

whenever the green aesthete starts to whoop
with horror at the house not made with hands
and when from vacuum cleaners and tinned soup
another pure theosophist demands

rebirth in other, less industrial stars
where huge towns thrust up in synthetic stone
and films, and sleek miraculous motor-cars
and celluloid and rubber are unknown;

when from his vegetable Sunday-school
emerges with the neatly maudlin phrase
still one more Nature poet, to rant and drool
about the 'standardization of the race'.

I see, stooping among her orchard trees
the old, sound Earth, gathering her windfalls in,
broad in the hams and stiffening at the knees,
pause, and I see her grave, malicious grin.

For there is no manufacturer competes
with her in the mass production of shapes and things.
Over and over she gathers and repeats
the cast of a face, a million butterfly wings.

She does not tire of the pattern of a rose,
her oldest tricks still catch us by surprise.
She cannot recall how long ago she chose
the streamlined hulls of fish, the snail's long eyes.

Love still pours into its ancient mould
the lashing seed that grows to man again
from whom by the same processes unfold
unending generations of living men.

She has standardized his ultimate needs and pains;
lost tribes in a lost language mutter in
his dreams: his science is tethered to their brains;
his guilt merely repeats Original Sin.

And beauty standing motionless before
her mirror sees behind her mile on mile
a long queue in an unknown corridor,
anonymous faces plastered with her smile.

A. D. HOPE

Statements about *Standardization*

☐ **1** This poem is not particularly 'poetic' in the conventional sense.

☐ **2** A. D. Hope is skeptical of critics of industrialized society.

☐ **3** The poet has a poor opinion of newspaper journalism.

☐ **4** Hope has little appreciation or respect for nature.

☐ **5** The poem's form echoes its theme.

☐ **6** The poem suggests that a human being is the ultimate standardized creature.

☐ **7** The poem suggests that nature is as standardized as modern industry.

☐ **8** Hope scoffs at human vanity.

☐ **9** The poem is well crafted; that is, it uses poetic devices purposefully and cleverly.

Follow the guidelines for consensus on pages 35-37.

ACTIVITY

Prayer Before Birth

I am not yet born; O hear me.
Let not the bloodsucking bat or the rat or the stoat or the
    clubfooted ghoul come near me.

I am not yet born; console me.
I fear that the human race may with tall walls wall me,
    with strong drugs dope me, with wise lies lure me,
        on black racks rack me, in blood-baths roll me.

I am not yet born; provide me
With water to dandle me, grass to grow for me, trees to talk
    to me, sky to sing to me, birds and a white light
        in the back of my mind to guide me.

I am not yet born; forgive me
For the sins that in me the world shall commit, my words
    when they speak me, my thoughts when they think me,
        my treason engendered by traitors beyond me,
            my life when they murder by means of my
                hands, my death when they live me.

I am not yet born; rehearse me
In the parts I must play and the cues I must take when
    old men lecture me, bureaucrats hector me, mountains
        frown at me, lovers laugh at me, the white
            waves call me to folly and the desert calls
                me to doom and the beggar refuses
                    my gift and my children curse me.

I am not yet born; O hear me,
Let not the man who is beast or who thinks he is God
    come near me.

I am not yet born; O fill me
With strength against those who would freeze my
    humanity, would dragoon me into a lethal automaton,
      would make me a cog in a machine, a thing with
        one face, a thing, and against all those
          who would dissipate my entirety, would
            blow me like thistledown hither and
              thither or hither and thither
                like water held in the
                  hands would spill me
Let them not make me a stone and let them not spill me.
Otherwise kill me.

LOUIS MACNEICE

Statements about *Prayer Before Birth*

This time, in your group, decide whether you agree or disagree with the following statements. Write 'A' or 'D' in the appropriate boxes as you reach consensus.

☐ **1** Louis MacNeice's poem is a total condemnation of life and living.

☐ **2** The poem is too cynical an exaggeration of life and living to be taken seriously.

☐ **3** Each verse could be said to have a particular theme. For example, the last verse can be summarized as a plan to retain one's individuality.

☐ **4** The poem is too prosaic (that is, too much like prose) to be seriously considered as poetry. (Consider rhyme, rhythm, form, use of language.)

ACTIVITY

Language and theme

Follow the guidelines for consensus on pages 35–37. Don't forget to make your individual rankings before any group discussion begins.

Do Not Go Gentle Into That Good Night

Do not go gentle into that good night,
Old age should burn and rave at close of day;
Rage, rage against the dying of the light.

Though wise men at their end know dark is right,
Because their words had forked no lightning they
Do not go gentle into that good night.

Good men, the last wave by, crying how bright
Their frail deeds might have danced in a green bay,
Rage, rage against the dying of the light.

Wild men who caught and sang the sun in flight,
And learn, too late, they grieved it on its way,
Do not go gentle into that good night.

Grave men, near death, who see with blinding sight
Blind eyes could blaze like meteors and be gay,
Rage, rage against the dying of the light.

And you, my father, there on the sad height,
Curse, bless, me now with your fierce tears, I pray.
Do not go gentle into that good night.
Rage, rage against the dying of the light.

DYLAN THOMAS

Statements about *Do Not Go Gentle*

- 1 Dylan Thomas wrote this poem about his angry father.
- 2 Thomas wrote this poem when contemplating his own death.
- 3 The poet believes that we rarely succeed in living our lives to the fullest.
- 4 The poet believes we should not be resigned to death or accept it peacefully; we should not fear it, but fight it.
- 5 The poem is based on one varying metaphor.
- 6 The poem's very consistent rhyme and tight form make it seem very contrived.
- 7 The poem is a forceful one. This force is derived from Thomas' use of harsh, monosyllabic words, repetition of key words and phrases, and the use of harsh alliteration.
- 8 Poets should communicate clearly. They should avoid using language in such unconventional ways as Thomas does here.

Mood and theme

Follow the guidelines for consensus on pages 35–37.

4
ACTIVITY

Ozymandias

I met a traveller from an antique land
Who said: Two vast and trunkless legs of stone
Stand in the desert . . . Near them, on the sand,
Half sunk, a shattered visage lies, whose frown,
And wrinkled lip, and sneer of cold command,
Tell that its sculptor well those passions read
Which yet survive, stamped on these lifeless things,
The hand that mocked them, and the heart that fed:
And on the pedestal these words appear:
'My name is Ozymandias, king of kings:
Look on my works, ye Mighty, and despair!'
Nothing beside remains. Round the decay
Of that colossal wreck, boundless and bare
The lone and level sands stretch far away.

PERCY BYSSHE SHELLEY

Statements about *Ozymandias*

☐ **1** The poet paints a complimentary picture of Ozymandias.

☐ **2** The word 'despair' in line 11 means that Ozymandias felt despair because he knew he could not keep his power forever.

☐ **3** The mood of the poem suggests that Ozymandias had regard for peasants, as, for example, the sculptor who carved his statue.

☐ **4** The image of the final three lines shows that the poet respects nature's supremacy.

☐ **5** The poem is essentially concerned with time's destructive power.

☐ **6** The poem's power lies in the subtle use of irony.

☐ **7** Shelley is as concerned with his craft (controlled use of form and poetic devices) as he is with his subject.

☐ **8** The movement of the poem helps to build up the mood.

☐ **9** The carefully chosen words dictate the mood of despair and futility in the poem.

5
ACTIVITY

Judging the poem

Follow the guidelines for discussion on pages 35–37.

In this exercise, the six participants are judges in a high school poetry competition. Below are the poems of the three finalists in the senior section.

Try to reach consensus, using whatever criteria you choose, on the first, second and third place winners.

When you have finished, and the observers have made their comments, compare your results with those of the other groups.

Who Will Take Grandma?

Who will take Grandma? Who will it be?
All of us want her—I'm sure you'll agree.
Let's call a meeting—let's gather the clan,
Let's get it settled as soon as we can.
In such a big family there's certainly one
Willing to give her a place in the sun.
Strange how we thought she would never wear out,
But see how she walks? It's arthritis, no doubt.
Her eyesight is faded, her memory is dim.
She's apt to insist on the silliest whim.
When people get older they become such a care,
She must have a home—but the question is where?
Remember the days when she used to be spry?

Baked her own cookies and made her own pie,
Helped us with lessons and tended our seams,
Kissed away troubles and mended our dreams?
Wonderful Grandma, we all loved her so,
One little corner is all she would need,
A shoulder to cry on, a Bible to read,
A chair by the window with the sun shining through
Some pretty spring flowers still covered in dew.
Who'll warm her with love so she won't mind the cold?
Oh, who will take Grandma now that she's old?
What? Nobody wants her!? . . . Oh yes, there is one,
Willing to give her a place in the sun,
Where she won't have to worry or wonder or doubt
And she won't be our problem to bother about.
Pretty soon now, God will give her a bed,
But who'll dry our tears, when Grandma is dead?

CRAIG REED
(STUDENT)

Eulogy

My poetry moved to town today.
He packed his own bags,
buckled the straps of rhyme and rhythm with a little help
from my friends
then ran away from home on the last train.
He won't return.

We went to the station to wave goodbye
but he had already adopted the strange stilted manner
                of the city,
and we were ignored.

He left a photograph
taken when he was a child,
but it faces the wall for I cannot look upon that round
                young face
without remembering the last time I saw him,
mechanical as the iron wheels turning him away.

I'd had hopes for him
as that sweet beguiling child—
now that he has left for the bright lights of image
I have nothing but
frustration at my own failure to raise him with
                sincerity,
to make him see beyond the flesh
beyond the fashion.

Never mind, he was not my only child.

NICOLE MATHIESON
(STUDENT)

The Achiever

Sunshine hustles like the stray ginger cat,
encircling me three times then gone to sit on the stairs
head facing the opposite direction, ignoring my pleas
for company just a little bit longer.

Two concrete squares plus two concrete squares equals four
Concrete squares, where's the couch grass?
One cloud plus one cloud equals two clouds and they alone
eclipse the sky. One bird plus one body of water, they together
create the ripples and the cat comes back but the sun will not, and

the concrete cracks but the blade of grass snaps and the
clouds separate, but now it's black—too late and water's not
and the bird's not either and the ripple has elapsed into
nothingness.

The concrete chips and the clouds disappear, but the sky isn't
anything and the grass even less and the dusk on the open eyes
sears and one solitary figure sits unobserving, dangling
legs and cold and it alone can't initiate the ripples, see
the sky, plant the grass and smash the concrete.

Ah but the cat's back and the sun's still on the run
That solitary figure now can.

SUSAN LEGGETT
(STUDENT)

4
Small group explorations

*A*s with a whole-class fish-bowl discussion, the aim when working in small groups is to use time effectively and efficiently. One of the most useful 'controls' over small group technique and performance is the observer. By noting individual and collective group behaviour, the observer can monitor, expose, and ultimately improve group performance through feedback which increases participant awareness of productive techniques and roles.

Small group guidelines

1 Form groups of about six. For each new activity appoint a chairperson to initiate, organise and co-ordinate your discussion.

2 Appoint a new observer for each new activity. Use copies of the fish-bowl checklist on page 24, in rotation with the two charts which follow: 'Critical incidents' and 'Who talks how much?'. Follow the suggestions for their use, and at the end of the discussion, give appropriate feedback.

   Observer sensitivity is essential if the group (and more importantly the individual) is to accept criticism in the manner in which it is intended—as an aid to improved group participation and productivity.

3 You may like to take on special roles, as were assumed for Fish-bowl 2 on page 31. Whether you follow these guidelines or not, though, each group member's contribution should be clearly apparent.

4 Some of the following explorations involve an activity component as well as discussion. Teacher direction will be needed here to decide where the observer role should start and finish. As well, when you feel your group is working well, you may occasionally choose to do without the observer.

Critical incidents—observer checklist

Note the critical incidents that occur in the group's development. Many of these are likely to occur in the first and last few minutes of the discussion.

Make enough notes in the space provided to be able to describe these incidents when you give your feedback. Look out for about half a dozen incidents of points such as these:

1 The group seems at a loss as to what to do.

2 A major decision is made about how to proceed.

3 A major change in group direction might have occurred if individuals had acted differently.

4 The method or pace of work suddenly changes.

5 Something occurs to boost the discussion along.

6 Something occurs which stifles the discussion.

Feedback: Observers and participants discuss together the incidents that occurred. Try to determine how positive incidents might be effected in the future; how negative incidents could be avoided.

Who talks how much?

Note the number of times each group member contributes to the discussion during its early, middle and late periods. Write the name of each group member in the spaces provided. Each time a person makes a contribution of *at least three words* make a mark in the appropriate box beside his or her name.

Number of contributions

Name	First period (5 minutes)	Second period (5 minutes)	Third period (5 minutes)
1			
2			
3			
4			
5			
6			

Feedback: Having discovered who talked the most, you could ban that student from speaking at all in your next discussion (he or she can write down any imperative thoughts!). At the end the banned student could report on how it felt to be silent, while the rest of you could discuss what difference it made when a usually talkative member was silent.

And having discovered who spoke least, you could draw out that student with questions and other encouragement to express himself or herself more in a subsequent discussion.

Or you could use your feedback in a different way: for example, it is reputed that boys dominate the talk in the classroom. You can use your own data to see if this is true. If your group is an exception, discuss why this might be so. If boys do dominate the talk, think about the reasons why.

Proving poetry is fun

ACTIVITY

Follow the small group guidelines on the preceding pages. Remember, whether or not you decide to take on roles, each member's contribution must be clearly apparent.

Your task is to devise a strategy for proving the statement: 'Poetry can be fun'.

After whatever discussion is necessary, come to a decision as to how you are to present your proof. It may be written, visual, oral or aural— or any combination of these.

Finally, prepare your 'proof' and present it to the class.

Themes and symbols

2 ACTIVITY

Follow the small group guidelines on pages 45-47, and as a group, decide how, why, and to what extent, the accompanying visual image could be considered a symbolic illustration of David Malouf's poem.

Epitaph for a Monster of Our Times

The age admires precision
and this man was precise
a passion for names and numbers
they say his only vice,

a kindly man with blue
and inoffensive eyes,
a public servant slightly
smaller than life size,

who sat at his desk a slave
to files and paper-clips
while children died and cities
burned at his fingertips,

a Caligula by proxy,
stiff-collared dispassionate,
whose crablike hand kept entry
of number name and date,

using the regulation
form, the official quill,
to sign with equal flourish
death-warrant, laundry bill;

an organization man
par excellence whom we
need only convict at last
of gross efficiency.

DAVID MALOUF

3 ACTIVITY

1 Read each of the following poems. Discuss each poem's possible theme or themes, and consider how illustrations could be used to represent them.

2 Explore magazines and newspapers for a possible visual symbolic representation of the theme or themes. (The illustration accompanying the Malouf poem was part of an advertisement in a daily newspaper.) Alternatively, you may find a suitable cartoon or make your own sketch; *any* visual medium will do.

3 Make a display of your results, and compare and discuss your illustrations with those of other groups.

Logic

Last year
My father died.
It stretched him out
And took his breath
Away clear.
It was so much it
Broke the back
Of reason.

When I find hoards
Of foreign coins,
Or see his books
And pills again,
I leave them back
And dust around those
Little jabs
Of pain.

ROSEMARY COWAN
(STUDENT)

Skull

Bloated my great grey mass
Is crazed with cracks; age
Has polished me like smooth glass.

In the brain, ideas hum into flight,
Through a hive of swarming laughter
To layered honeycombs of thought
But no mind flaps up from the skull;
Merely the motions of a well-built cage
Responding blindly to the brain's pull.

Yet, hollow globe of bone,
I grin wordlessly long ages after
My fragile tenants are gone.

ARNOLD HUNT
(STUDENT)

The Commercial Hotel

Days of asphalt–blue and gold
murmurous with stout and flies,
lorries bought, allotments sold,

and recent heroes, newly old,
stare at their beer with bloating eyes.
Days of asphalt–blue and gold

dim to saloon bars, where unfold
subtleties of enterprise,
lorries bought, allotments sold,

where, with fingers burnt, the bold
learn to be indirect, and wise.
Days of asphalt–blue and gold

confirm the nation in its mould
of wages, contract and supplies,
lorries bought, allotments sold,

and the brave, their stories told,
age and regard, without surmise,
days of asphalt–blue and gold
lorries bought, allotments sold.

LES MURRAY

Piano

Softly, in the dusk, a woman is singing to me;
Taking me back down the vista of years, till I see
A child sitting under the piano, in the boom of the
      tingling strings
And pressing the small, poised feet of a mother
      who smiles as she sings.

In spite of myself, the insidious mastery of song
Betrays me back, till the heart of me weeps to belong
To the old Sunday evenings at home, with winter
      outside
And hymns in the cosy parlour, the tinkling piano
      our guide.

So now it is vain for the singer to burst into clamour
With the great black piano appassionato. The glamour
Of childish days is upon me, my manhood is cast
Down in the flood of remembrance, I weep like a child
      for the past.

D. H. LAWRENCE

London

I wander through each chartered street,
Near where the chartered Thames does flow,
And mark in every face I meet
Marks of weakness, marks of woe.

In every cry of every Man,
In every Infant's cry of fear,
In every voice, in every ban,
The mind-forged manacles I hear.

How the Chimney-sweeper's cry
Every blackening Church appalls;
And the hapless Soldier's sigh
Runs in blood down Palace walls.

But most through midnight streets I hear
How the youthful Harlot's curse
Blasts the new born Infant's tear,
And blights with plagues the Marriage hearse.

WILLIAM BLAKE

Tabula Rasa

Accustomed to the graffiti of playground
and public place, the free enterprising
defacements of commerce, and the pulsing
repetitious overload of the private screen,
their nightblind eyes turn shortsighted,
blur astigmatically even as I scribble
my words on an untechnological blackboard.

Each day the marks of my trade are erased
from that gentle surface, though if you look
closely enough, you can just see the faintest
of philosophies there, one shadowy day on
another. Let but a decade pass, and their eyes
will light with recognition of me, who wrote
those chalk-white words into their minds.

ROSS CLARK

Exploring meaning

The following poems are presented because their message, or 'story', could be said to be puzzling or elusive. Such poems can provide a real point of contention between poets, readers and critics. While some believe that a poem should be universally clear and comprehensible, others believe it is up to the individual to explore the poem for his or her own interpretation. Others, again, feel that one can simply 'experience' a poem without worrying too much about its precise meaning or message.

Is it enough that a poem simply *sounds* poetic and makes some sort of sensuous impression on you, or should it make complete sense as well?

1 Follow the guidelines on pages 45–47, and consider the attitudes and questions raised above in your small groups. (Consensus would probably be out of the question!)

2 Having completed this general discussion, consider each of the following poems and share your opinions and interpretations.

4

ACTIVITY

Rose

Red rose, red rhythmed rose
Red tooth-mugged ripe rhythmed rose
Is pulsing, quick on my rose-shelf.

The room seems full of petals.
Red, red, red rose petals, and
They sing upon the floor.
My eyes, perhaps, are petals:
Red with love, pulsating: petals.

O there is a young, blush, red rose
Vivid in my tooth-mug:
     no one has seen her
Save me:
   my eyes which, like rose's
Red eye, she brightens and bares.

JAMES LOXLEY
(STUDENT)

And No Bird Sings

the music is over
its time now
for silence, for
listening to the wind, the
rain. say nothing,
that would be wrong, speaking
is words no more, is not poems.
humanity is ghosts and politics,
is hopeless sentiment.

its time now
to say nothing
time for the wind

time for the green pastures
the quiet waters

time for
Cain or a serpent
or a miracle

MICHAEL DRANSFIELD

Love So Surprise?

When in the wind is the where?
With the blue-eyes, the you-eyes,
And with the so wind in your hair
So golden, so random surprise?

Whither your lips so red,
Which meet mine in when and in where?
What words my lips so said
So lost in the random-wind there?

So love-lost in purple heather, or
Who else in the world so fair
Or cheeks so smooth, or law
Of Nature surprise in the care?

When the You and the wind in the heather
With me, lips, words of Us love?
Is Nature random, so together
The Us and the so clouds above?

Is love in your eyes, You so fair?
Above us the random cloud wise?
Whither the random when and the where?
My nature—love you—so surprise?

JON HARLEY
(STUDENT)

Served With Notice

Noticing in the morning paper that this
cafe is to come down to give rise
to thirty-one storeys, I enter (to give it a lift
while I may); noticing that ivy in the window
is not plastic and shoots a leafbud
minutely shaped as a figure with bowed head:

and noticing how the smoke of my fag
trembles in a wind of passage although my hand
is steady, I notice furtively I am alone
for ever as always I was since I began
sitting up to take notice. Across the road

the portals of the Melbourne Club evict
a bad smell under the nose that gives me
notice I am noticeably unfit to be admitted
and I goes berserk (furtively), ducking
under a tenuous connection with the fact
that *all* the buildings are to come down.

Read about it, Read about it.
Club Membah's Wife Stays Put.
Refuses to High-Rise.

They're shooting from both sides.
Me and the ivy bows low
and goes.
Having paid.

ANNE ELDER

La Belle Dame Sans Merci

O what can ail thee Knight at arms,
  Alone and palely loitering?
The sedge has withered from the Lake
  And no birds sing!

O what can ail thee Knight at arms,
  So haggard, and so woe-begone?
The squirrel's granary is full
  And the harvest's done.

I see a lily on thy brow,
  With anguish moist and fever dew,
And on thy cheek a fading rose
  Fast withereth too—

I met a Lady in the Meads
  Full beautiful, a faery's child;
Her hair was long, her foot was light,
  And her eyes were wild—

I made a garland for her head,
  And bracelets too, and fragrant Zone;
She look'd at me as she did love
  And made sweet moan—

I set her on my pacing steed,
  And nothing else saw all day long;
For sidelong would she bend and sing
  A faery's song—

She found me roots of relish sweet,
  And honey wild, and manna dew;
And sure in language strange she said
  I love thee true—

She took me to her elfin grot,
  And there she wept and sigh'd full sore,
And there I shut her wild wild eyes
  With kisses four.

And there she lulled me asleep,
  And there I dream'd, Ah Woe betide!
The latest dream I ever dreamt
  On the cold hill side.

I saw pale Kings, and Princes too,
  Pale warriors, death-pale were they all;
They cried 'La belle Dame sans Merci
  Hath thee in thrall.'

I saw their starv'd lips in the gloam
  With horrid warning gaped wide,
And I awoke and found me here
  On the cold hill's side.

And this is why I sojourn here
  Alone and palely loitering;
Though the sedge is withered from the Lake,
  And no birds sing.

JOHN KEATS

The Door

Somewhere in my head is a door.
Sealed. Invisible. Impossible
to prize and wrench
open. My head is a clean place.
I keep it tidy and neat. I need a
habitable environment for my
nice and neat little self.

Behind the door is another world.
Demons whirl there, gods rage and die and are
reborn. Flowers and gardens erupt
in frantic profusion. Processions of faces
loom out of darkness, hands grip my throat.

From the white peace of my head
I long for the door.
I am Alice, Pandora, I fling my fingers across
immaculate plaster—smooth emptiness.
The door has vanished—
never existed. I weep in my clean white
empty house.

Nights without warning the door will swing
open again letting forth to devour me
swarms of shrieking bats
in hideous glory.

JENI COUZYN

Poetic devices

In chapter 1 we looked briefly at different types of imagery—**simile,
metaphor** and **personification** (page 9)—and explored the sound
imagery of **onomatopoeia** (page 12). These are all poetic devices. The
following notes present some other basic poetic terms and devices
(many of which you are probably already familiar with).

NOTES

Form

In poetry, 'form' refers to the pattern, or structure of the poem, for
example a ballad, a sonnet, or free verse. Many of the various poetic
forms are described on pages 71-73.

Rhyme

Rhyme is the repetition, usually at the end of lines, of similar or identical sounds.

Rhythm

The movement, or rhythm, of the lines, is achieved by the regular or
recurrent pattern of emphasised sounds. The rhythm in Robert Browning's *How They Brought the Good News from Ghent to Aix* strongly
echoes the subject of the poem: a mad gallop across the countryside:

I sprang to the stirrup, and Joris, and he;
I galloped, Dirck galloped, we galloped all three;

Alliteration

Alliteration is the repetition of consonants, especially at the beginning of words. It is used to emphasise or intensify an image, as in this example by Edmund Spenser:

The *b*lazing *b*rightness of her *b*eauties *b*eame,

Consonance

Used for similar effect to alliteration, consonance is the repetition of consonants at the *end* of syllables.

Assonance

Assonance is the rhyming, or repetition, of vowel sounds, for example in Thomas Campion's:

Sing thou *smoothly* with thy *beauty's*
Silent *music*.

Tone

Like mood, tone conveys the overall attitude, spirit or character of the poem.

Rosemary Cowan was a major award winner in a poetry competition. While the following two examples of her work have been judged to be excellent poetry, they are not obviously or overtly 'poetic' in terms of rhyme or rhythm.

5
ACTIVITY

Peace of Mind

I
You who have not seen death,
Say you would kill with ease
To keep your long-won freedom.
But war veterans hesitate to
Tumble a man again into the
Heavy slop of a mud grave.
And so would rather cry
In peace behind white walls.
Today I have heard a soldier's
Latest scream, when he had thought
Himself blown up to heaven,
Fell to earth once more and
Stumbled on feet no longer his.

II
I have known a little girl
So charred and frozen, like
The day the lava spilled
Over all Pompeii and kept
Its people nameless; her mother

Only knew her for her size
And height. Yet as the small
Coffin wended in at the
Front door, the mother rushed
Out through the back and
Silent tears fell on the lawn.

III
I daresay you know the other
Anguish too. The black figure
Backtracks across the Diamond,
Later, out of den, the plastic
Smears his features. The gunman's
Wife who gave herself a chill reception
In the stream; the next dawn found
Her face down, her nightdress was
Flecked with ravening foam.

IV
I daresay you might still kill,
Forgetting the bin-lid rattle of
Machine-guns that haunts our dreams.
And nightmare flickers like the
Flames past our windows, whispering
We are never free until the
Earth has rolled us round and
Let us sleep secure.

Borderlines

He saw them right enough.
His mind went Border Patrol
As he searched for his licence.
But in his heart thumped
A peculiar pain as they
Swarmed around the headlamps.
He didn't make a move, not yet,
He wasn't sure if he'd heard
Alright and anyway the cold
Steady drizzle put him off
On a night when he should
Be by a good turf fire.
And so they opened the cab
Door to wrench him out
In one firm, cloying grasp.
He looked and thought to
See a hardened Catholic face
With black beret and sleeked eye
But saw instead a blond man.
Disinterested and with a green
Muffler. One shot blasted
Him into the sodden ditch.
They found him later and

His cattle truck; they cleaned
Him up so people admired his
Neat grey coffin suit but
Avoided looking at the
Mess where his face had been.

ROSEMARY COWAN
(STUDENT)

1 In your groups, read the poems aloud several times until you arrive at an understanding of their content and intention.

2 Observe the small group guidelines on pages 45–46 and discuss the poems.

Your discussion should consider these questions as well as any others you may want to raise.
• what feelings do these two poems create?
• what tone is the writer adopting?
• what is the poet saying about death?
• what images struck you?
• what can you say about the rhyme and rhythm?

3 Compare your findings as a whole class group.

Poetry or prose?

Much of the poetry of the last fifty or sixty years has been written in *free verse*, or in a combination of free and metrical verse.

The free verse form arose to overcome the often sentimental, smooth and obvious versification of late nineteenth and early twentieth century poetry. Free verse has many critics. Abandoning, as it does, rhyme, metre, and the pattern of stresses and syllables, it is often accused of being prose masquerading as poetry. In other words, critics say it is merely prose divided into lines of varying lengths.

NOTES
Metrical verse

Metrical verse is based on *metre*—the particular pattern of sounds that a poet uses to create an appropriate or musical rhythm. The pattern is formed by the combination of *stressed* (emphasised) and *unstressed* syllables within a line, for example:

A thing of beauty is a joy forever

This pattern of an unstresed syllable (◡) followed by a stressed syllable (/) is called *iambic* metre, the most commonly used metre in English poetry. Each unit of the pattern (◡/) is called a *foot*. Looking again at the example of rhythm on page 57, the basic pattern is *anapestic* (◡◡/):

I sprang to the stirrup, and Joris, and he;
I galloped, Dirck galloped, we galloped all three

There are many other metres formed by different combinations of stressed and unstressed syllables.

Free verse

Free verse has no rigid, formal structure or metre. Its writers strive for balance and rhythm within the poem as a whole, rather than within each line or stanza. Each line is written to evoke the mood or thought of the moment rather than to conform to an established pattern. Do not confuse free verse with blank verse metre.

Blank verse metre

Blank verse is unrhymed verse but it does have a regular metre. It is often used for narrative and dramatic verse, and is often composed in *iambic pentameter* (a line of *five* iambic feet). For example 'A thing of beauty is a joy forever' has five iambic feet.

6
ACTIVITY

Your task, as fair critics, is to make a distinction between good free verse—poetry—and poor, prosaic attempts at free verse.
Here is a checklist of criteria to help you decide:
• The poem has, if not a regular pattern, at least a form of its own.
• Good free verse has brief echoes of metrical verse—a mixture of recognizable metrical feet.
• An element of rhythm can be found in the phrasing of thought and images.
• The irregular rhythm and the pauses are meaningful. They echo or fit the sense of what is being said.

Following the small group guidelines on pages 45–46, and using the above criteria alone (that is, ignore devices such as imagery which prose writers are free to use too) judge the following poems. Are they poetry, or prose masquerading as poetry?

if there are any heavens my mother will (all by herself) have
one. It will not be a pansy heaven nor
a fragile heaven of lilies-of-the-valley but
it will be a heaven of blackred roses

my father will be (deep like a rose
tall like a rose)

standing near my

(swaying over her
silent)
with eyes which are really petals and see

nothing with the face of a poet really which
is a flower and not a face with
hands
which whisper
This is my beloved my

                    (suddenly in sunlight
he will bow,

& the whole garden will bow)

                                        e. e. cummings

The Way We Live Now

". . . at the end of the earth
where existence is most easy
Snoe never falls there and no wild storms
disturb the sweetly flowing days:
only the soothing breezes of the West Wind
drift in each day from Ocean, bearing
constant refreshment for the inhabitants . . ."

                    (*The Odyssey*, Book IV)

1
Here the talk's of flowering annuals,
investments.

Ah, the *richness* of our soil!

Each morning automatic sprinklers bless
all that's governable and nice;
sleek insects fatten on our ceaseless flowers;
glistening motors roam the land.

In our desirable brick-and-tiles
we dream of real estate.

2

Pursued by industrial suburbs—
"the concrete evidence of our progress"—
the bush has fled to the hills. Those hills are alive
with machines, developers, dust. Beyond,
our country lies, wide
and open.

We are, we often feel, living
on the edge of something good.

3

Nothing disturbs us.

Winds from Africa and Indian waves
bear each day to our long white shore
only what we most admire: fashions,
technology, and rich strangers as neat as
beetles who smile at our
simple friendliness.

4

Yes, we like it here.

Sometimes the shrewdest of us find the time,
after the gardening, before television,
sipping beer on enclosed verandahs,
to speculate on the future.

WILLIAM GRONO

The Necklace

A solitary woman squats by the roadside
threading fabled dreams
in the colour of her beads.
Cedar and laurel seeds notch
the rosary of patience with blue fragments
of sky forever arrowed in her eyes.

Her fingers scurry in the granary,
sifting the precious hoard hidden
in a brown paper bag. Silently and accurately
she knows the beads one by one
slipping furtively down
the string of her days.
Who will buy the simple geometry
of her life?

The sun lowers her bowed head
petrifying thoughts into rock and sand
but the hands keep praying
the litany for grace in the desert.

SILVANA GARDNER

Friendships

The teacher forced alliances—
Tried to teach "awareness".
We were made to expose likes and dislikes, thoughts and feelings.
We played name-games, face-games, voice-games,
Formed outer shells of friendship:
Thin skins, surface gloss, shallow shine,
Veneer!
Plywood performances and laminex laughter,
A furniture-display arranged
By her, for her.
And then she left.

The polish dulled . . .
Smeared with embarrassment.
Each face a flimsy chair
Separate
No more the matching suite.
Tentative questions emerged.
I observed, listened, thought and dropped cautious words.
ONE girl was eager, alert and witty.
I edged closer . . . and conversed.
Similar likes! Similar dislikes! Similar opinions!
There WERE irritations
But minor.

Minor became major.
When someone else appeared she reflected THEIR ideas . . .
A mirror.
Changing to fit her company
As a beanbag moulds around a rear.
She did NOT think for herself—
She meekly just agreed . . .
A coat-hanger for others' whims.
VERY pretty upholstery,
Comfortable padding,
But no firm foundation.
No sound support from supple springs
Thus crumpling under pressure.

I'm secure, I'm dramatic, I'm aggressive.
I need someone who bounces back . . .

A trampoline?

ERICA FRYBERG

Church Grounds

Bright Sunday at lunchtime
in the grimy suburb:
the presbytery's at prayers
or eating, and the nuns also—
I shortcut through

their schoolyard, down the steps
beside the church, onto
asphalt marked out
for basketball, in orange,
with the metal goals
swung down by the kids, the nets
torn and hanging like
stranded seaweed.
The garbage cans are tipped over
by them or
the stray dogs. Down here
under brick walls
(the colour of cold baked meat)
a flock of pigeons
walking. Nothing else around.
The pigeons pedal off in all
directions, eyes backwards—they
keep pecking
at the air in front of them
as they go. Tick, tick, tick.
If they're not
stabbing at the ground
for crumbs, they're keeping on
into nothing;
that's their whole life . . .

ROBERT GRAY

Exploring the total poem

ACTIVITY

1 In your groups explore *Initiation* and come to an understanding of it
as best you can.

Initiation

In shadowed and red–curtained room
My father talked towards his death
While birds made morning in the sky
And children laughed his death a lie
And each sun on the window-pane
Asked him would they meet again?

And I sat with him in the room,
Listened, nodded, laughed and talked
And brought him living words that mocked
The lonely, leafless road he walked.
He watched us distant, passing by.
Alone my father had to die.

Words withered in the barren breath.
Friends gathered in his lonely place,
Stood hope to hope and could not stop
Death closing on my father's face.
Love's bleeding fingers could not break
The way my father had to take.

Oh how time held us in his fist
And forced us to a helpless close,
Took a night, a room, a drifting mist
And nailed them on my father's life.
The cancer rotting in the lung
Cared not how many hands were wrung.

Then let me not take sackcloth for my grief
Or hang the hungry lashes with my tears.
This man went as quiet as a leaf,
Dumb as a lily in the singing years.
The wind in harebells will ring loud enough.
Nothing. Nothing. Nothing is enough.

WILLIAM MCILVANNEY

2 Prepare a list of questions that your group may have about the
poem. Broadly, your questions should fall into three categories:
   • theme and content
   • poetic qualities
   • appeal.

3 As each group presents its questions, the teacher and the rest of the
class listen, respond and make contributions where appropriate.

II
Reading and writing

5
Investigations

*T*he activities in this chapter may be approached individually, in pairs or in small groups.

You will need a good supply of poetry books and anthologies, and where possible, it will be a good idea to have half of the class in the library (on a rotational basis) for some lessons. The decreased numbers will improve opportunities for student/teacher discussion, while those in the library will have access to a greater range of poetry resources.

A poem should . . .

A poem should be motionless in time
As the moon climbs   Archibald MacLeish

Poetry can sting the conscience or shock us into awareness.

Poetry can awaken our senses of touch, taste, smell, sight and hearing.

A poem should not mean
But be.   Archibald MacLeish

Poetry can build a dream world into which, momentarily, we may escape.

I think poetry is written mostly for pleasure, by which I mean the pleasure of pain, horror, anguish and awe, as well as the pleasure of beauty, music and the act of living.   Kenneth Slessor

Poetry is the language of the imagination.   William Hazlitt

I have said that poetry is the spontaneous overflow of powerful feelings.   William Wordsworth

Poetry is what makes me laugh or cry or yawn, what makes my toenails twinkle, what makes me want to do this or that or nothing.
Dylan Thomas

Prose: Words in their best order
Poetry: The best words in their best order   Samuel Taylor Coleridge

When in public poetry should take off its clothes and wave to the nearest person in sight; it should be seen in the company of thieves and lovers rather than that of journalists and publishers.   Brian Patten

Frozen, as in ice, years past
That moment lingers still—
Silent, yet alive,
The moment lives for evermore.   Student

Poetry can create a picture of the world, the spirit of an age.

To see a world in a Grain of Sand
And Heaven in a Wild Flower,
Hold Infinity in the palm of your hand
And eternity in an hour.   William Blake

Poetry is the record of the best and happiest moments of the best and happiest minds.   Percy Bysshe Shelley

Poetry is the synthesis of hyacinths and biscuits.   Carl Sandburg

The principal object proposed in these poems was to choose incidents and situations from common life, and to relate or describe them throughout, as far as was possible, in a selection of language really used by men, and, at the same time, to throw over them a certain colouring of imagination, whereby ordinary things should be presented to the mind in an unusual aspect.   William Wordworth

Anything can be poetry, from a letter to the editor or a recipe to an epic.   Ted Berrigan

Poetry is a celebration of life's possibilities.   David Holbrook

One writes when one wants to get something off one's chest.
T. S. Eliot

Poetry seeks to express a peculiar fusion of ideas and emotions which are normally on the edge of consciousness, or even beyond it.
T. R. Henn

Poetry can stimulate the imagination so that we make connections between objects that we have never connected before.

From this collection of statements about what poetry is, or ought to be, choose at least ten and find a poem to support each one. Write a few lines to support your choice of poem in each case.

ACTIVITY

Alternatively, each class member could choose a different statement to illustrate and a class anthology of '*A poem should . . .*' could be collated.

Poetic form

Form, in poetry, refers to the pattern, or structure, of the poem. We have seen that free verse is a particular poetic form; in the notes that follow several more forms are introduced.

NOTES

Ballad

Traditionally, a ballad is a folk-song which tells a story of love, adventure, tragedy; of fair deeds and foul. It is characterized by a simple stanza form, simple language and regular rhyme and rhythm. The *traditional ballad* is highly dramatic, using suspense and dialogue to gradually reveal the full story. Deliberate, rhythmical repetition aids this dramatic effect.

The traditional ballad form has passed down through the centuries—through the more refined literary ballads of the Romantic poets, to the ballads of contemporary poets and song-writers. Its simple, rhythmical form makes it a popular vehicle for propaganda and protest songs.

Elegy

An elegy is a dignified poem on a serious subject, usually the death of a loved one. It may be in any actual verse form—it is the content and *melancholic tone* which classify the poem as elegiac. Many examples can be found in eighteenth century classical poetry.

Epic

An epic is a long, serious, narrative poem relating a heroic journey, quest or adventure of great significance. Supernatural beings often

figure in such poems, guiding the progress of the central heroic character. The lines of an epic are of uniform length without division into stanzas; it is not a common contemporary form.

In the *mock-epic*, or *mock-heroic*, poem high-sounding expression, long words, exaggeration and anti-climax are used to satirize frivolous events and self-important people. Pope and Dryden frequently wrote in this form.

Ode

A dignified and emotional rhyming address to a person or object deemed worthy of such attention, the classical ode has a regular stanza pattern, is often written in three separate parts, and is intended to be read aloud. Romantic poets made much use of this form.

Song-lyric

As you might imagine from its title, the song-lyric is intended to be sung. It is simple in language and form, and uses assonance, consonance, alliteration and repetition for musical effect. Its themes are usually universal and emotive.

Lyric

Originally intended to be sung (eg the ballad lyric), hence the title, a lyric is a short, spontaneous poem with a recurring stanza and a particularly subjective quality. All poetry of thought and emotion can be termed lyric.

Pastoral

A pastoral depicts an artificially simple and idyllic rural scene; peopled by shepherds and shepherdesses. It has no fixed metrical or stanzaic conventions.

Dramatic monologue

In a dramatic monologue the poet (or rather, the character created) relates a dramatic incident to a silent listener or audience. It is a one-way conversation which affords the listener (or reader) insight into the character or temperament of the speaker. It is intensely dramatic in impact.

Sonnet

A sonnet is a very structured, disciplined poem of fourteen lines with a set rhyme pattern. It is often written in *iambic pentameter* (a verse line of ten syllables with every second syllable being stressed—refer to page 60 for a fuller explanation of syllables and stresses).

There are three main sonnet forms: Petrarchan, Shakespearian and Spenserian:

• The Petrarchan sonnet has a rhyming pattern of *abbaabba/cdecde* (that is *a* rhymes with *a*, *b* rhymes with *b*). The first eight lines (*octave*) present the ideas of the sonnet; the final six lines (*sestet*) complete the idea or make a comment on it.

- The rhyming pattern of the Shakespearian sonnet is *abab/cdcd/efef/gg*. It is composed of three *quatrains* (two pairs of rhyming lines), followed by a *couplet* (one pair of rhyming lines) which consolidates the poem's theme.
- The Spenserian sonnet follows the Shakespearian pattern except that the rhyme scheme is *abab/bebe/cdcd/ee*.

ACTIVITY

1 Using the notes provided above, find an example of each poetic form described from available anthologies.

2 Choose one form and imitate it in a poem of your own.

Thinking themes through

ACTIVITY

For this activity you will need a good supply of poetry books and anthologies. If possible, have half the class in the library.

1 Choose a theme which interests you: progress, peace, death, war, suburbia, modern living, happiness, love, childhood, conflict, friendship—the list is endless.

2 Find and read at least six poems (more if you are working as a pair or a small group) that reflect your particular theme.

3 Write out each poem on a separate sheet, recording also the name of the poet, the source and the page number.

4 Write a report to document and analyse the different aspects of the themes as treated in the different poems by different poets.

Reading Steve Turner

Steve Turner may not be a poet who is well known to you but he is well represented in this book and always receives an enthusiastic response when he reads his poetry in public. The poem printed below may give you some insight into the way Turner thinks and writes.

7/8 Of the Truth And Nothing But The Truth

If you are sitting comfortably
I suspect I am not giving you
the truth.
I am leaving you two poems
short of disagreement
so that you can remark upon
the likeness of our minds.
I am being kind.
I am giving you truth
in linctus form—strawberry flavour.
I am being unkind.
I am ignoring the correct dosage.

I want to be liked.
That's my trouble
I want to be agreed with.
I know you all like strawberry,
I quite like it myself.
It's nothing but the truth
but it's not the whole truth.

No one admires the whole truth.
No one ever applauds.
It takes things too far.
It's nice but where would
you put it?
People who neglect the strawberry
flavouring, do not get asked back.
They get put in their place,
with nails if necessary.

You will also find the following poems in the book.

When you have studied his poetry, take a look at these ten statements about it.
(If you can get hold of his 1983 collected edition called "Up to Date", published by Hodder this will help your work but it is not essential.)

1 Steve Turner may be witty but he rarely says anything very important.

2 His poetry is full of highly original images.

3 No other poet I know captures life in the busy late twentieth century quite like Turner.

4 His work is simple and direct but that means a single reading is always more than enough.

5 Turner's great talent is for the unpredictable.

6 His poetry has the immense advantage of forcing you to think.

7 Too often he fails to develop his ideas or his poems as fully as he might.

8 Whatever you think of his poetry, it sticks in the mind.

9 Turner has worked as a journalist and it shows. Some of his writing is not really poetry, it is propaganda.

10 Writers have a responsibility to think about what they say and Steve Turner is one who has taken his responsibility to heart.

1 Choose two of the statements with which you agree and write down why you agree, using the poems as evidence.

2 Choose two of the statements with which you disagree and show from the poems why you believe them to be wrong.

3 Divide into small groups to share your opinions.

4 Once you have heard each other, decide on the statement that the group agrees with most wholeheartedly and collect your evidence to defend that opinion.

   Secondly, decide on the one statement that the group feels is most misguided and collect the evidence that supports your opinion.

5 Have a session in which each group reports its findings and the whole class has an opportunity to comment.

4
ACTIVITY

Investigating the poet

Poets are people first and poets second. It would be hard for their poetry not to reflect the sort of people they are and the life experiences they've had. The poets listed below engaged in the following occupations at one time or another:

Dorothy Hewett	university lecturer, playwright
Bruce Dawe	petrol pump attendant, labourer, postie
John Manifold	tramp
Robyn Rowland	psychologist
Colin Thiele	principal of a Teachers' Centre
Bill Reed	blacksmith
Patti Smith	rock singer
Kenneth Slessor	war correspondent
Roger McGough	member of a pop group
William Shakespeare	theatre owner, playwright
Wilfred Owen	soldier
John Donne	clergyman
T.S. Eliot	clerk
Steve Turner	journalist

5
ACTIVITY

According to the resources available, choose a poet whom you would like to know more about—as a person and a poet. Your teacher will also be able to supply a list of possibilities.

1 Read as much as you can about your chosen poet's life and poetry.

2 Write a report explaining to what extent your poet's work could be said to reflect his or her life, experiences and beliefs.

3 Review your chosen poet's work, both thematically and stylistically:
   • **Thematically**—as well as content, include feeling, tone and the intention of the work.
   • **Stylistically**—include such aspects as form, poetical devices, imagery, figures of speech and language.

OR

Prepare a poetry reading of your poet's work to present to the class. The reading should include introductory comments about the poet and his or her life.

Appreciating the total poem

To wholly appraise and appreciate a poem, we need to consider two questions: *what* is the poet saying and *how* is he or she saying it?

What is the poet saying?

- Is the poem a story, an event, an experience, a 'slice of life', a description, an exhortation, a farce, a fantasy? Something else?

- Does the poem have a particular theme? How significant or original is it? How narrow, biased or broad is its treatment? Is it a personal, particular or universal view of the theme?

- Is it a contemporary issue or a timeless one? Is it about life, living, or the general human condition?

- Is the poet's intention clearly apparent? Was it worth saying, in your view?

- Did the poem strike a particular chord with you? Did it increase your awareness, broaden your experience of human life and nature, of the world in any way? Did it move you, excite you, anger you, contradict previously held ideas or beliefs?

How is it being said?

Consider the poem's overall:

Mood and Feeling
- Is there a particular mood? How is it created? (Consider language and rhythm in particular.)
- What are you moved to feel? How are these feelings engendered or fostered?

Tone
- Is the poet speaking in a particular tone of voice? What is this tone and how is it evident?
- Does the poet display any particular attitude to the reader? Is this effective, intended, functional?

Impact and Impression
- Did the poem have impact? Was it impressive, powerful, moving, surprising, thought-provoking, unsettling, enjoyable? None of these?
- Were you left unmoved, or with a negative impression?

When you are looking at the effect that the poem has on you, it might be worth bearing in mind some of these specific areas.

Imagery
- aural, visual, tactile
- simile, metaphor, personification

Sound
- assonance, consonance, alliteration, onomatopoeia
- perfect rhyme, half-rhyme, near rhyme
- movement and rhythm

Form

- Is the poem written in a traditional poetic form?
- Is the form functional and effective or merely poetically artificial? Does it seem strained or contrived?
- Is it a creative or original form or shape?

ACTIVITY

Use the guidelines and considerations above to write an appreciation of one of the poems that follow. You should be able to write at least one paragraph on *what* the poet is saying and two or three paragraphs on *how* it is said.

Don't slavishly answer all the questions or follow all the headings. They will not all be relevant. Equally, something of relevance to your chosen poem may not have been mentioned and you will need to add it.

The Searchers

(*The* Loch Ard *was wrecked off the coast near Port Campbell in 1878, drowning fifty of the passengers and crew.*)

But cold out there and dark, and after all
to seek for death is not a pleasant task;
the searchers' sandprints shortened with the dusk,
their lantern-comfort tentative and pale . . .

Cocooned from cold, high-collared to the wind,
the searchers peered across the wintered dark,
while tots of rum built up a frail bulwark
against what lung-choked jetsam they might find.

Each step was hesitant, vivid surmise
etching sharp portraits of the nameless dead;
shadows wore bones, each rock a dripping head
and every rockpool glinted with blank eyes.

A body joined the search: the huddled men
were cupped around warm talk of going back
when a long tongue of tide thrust out the slack
bread-white and bloated offering, like phlegm

from the sea's throat. The skin was alumed hide
and bloodless blue the stains their fingers left.
They dragged the naked body to a cleft
of rock, and wedged it from the morning tide,

then left it there and climbed the sullen rise
of sandstone cliff. So Mitchell, migrant, lay
his first night in the new land and, next day,
greeted the sun he'd sought, with salt-blind eyes.

B. A. BREEN

Five Hundred Million Pounds

The Earl of Grosvenor
has five hundred million pounds.
He is honeymooning in Hawaii.
He has five hundred million pounds
and he still has to honeymoon
in the world.
He has married Natalia.
She is not my sort of girl.
Five hundred million pounds
and he marries someone
who is not my sort of girl.
The Earl of Grosvenor
carries a black case
in his right hand.
Five hundred million pounds
and he still has to carry
a black case in his right hand.
It is probably heavy
He will probably sweat.
Damp patches will form
beneath his arms
as if he were a construction worker
or an unemployed gentleman
carrying a black case.
I expect his shoes hurt sometimes.
I expect he forgets his handkerchief.
I expect he wonders whether Natalia
really loves him.

I expect he wonders what it would be like
to have only four hundred and fifty
million pounds.
The Earl of Grosvenor takes off.
He wonders whether the engines will catch fire.
He knows you can't pay engines off.
He knows that the ocean is indifferent to millionaires.
Five hours in the air and he is restless.
Five hundred million pounds and he is restless.

STEVE TURNER

Atlantic Beach

It stretches out in
Summer; a white-gold
Band of loving and
Promise of sun.
The clean grit feeling
Of familiar sand
In every fold of rug
And body. The noise
Seems false, rising out
On mirage airbeds.
Little cat waves lap
Up the children,
Oiled, heavy heat
Takes a living sap.

Only the banshee
Gulls scream true. In dim
Winter dawns a face
Pock-marked by joggers
Heels just too fast or
Slow for fluid grace.
And quiet men walk with
Dogs to Barmouth in
Flurry of salt and
Fur. Sea binds the land
In grey-blue serge, seams
White, split by the rocks,
I sit with stick
And stir my dreams.

ROSEMARY COWAN (STUDENT)

At My Grandmother's

An afternoon late summer, in a room
shuttered against the bright envenomed leaves:
an underwater world, where time like water
was held in the wide arms of a gilded clock
and my grandmother, turning in the still Sargasso
of memory, wound out her griefs and held
a small boy prisoner to weeds and corals
while summer leaked its daylight through his head.

I feared that room: the parrot screeching soundless
in its dome of glass, the faded butterflies
like jewels pinned against a sable cloak;
and my grandmother winding out the skeins I held
like trickling time between my outstretched arms.

Feared most of all the stiff bejewelled fingers
pinned at her throat or moving on grey wings
from word to word; and feared her voice that called
down from their gilded frames the ghosts of children
who played at hoop and ball, whose spindrift faces

(the drowned might wear such smiles) looked out across
the wrack and debris of the years to where
a small boy sat, as they once sat, and held
in the wide ache of his arms all time like water,
and watched the old grey hands wind out his blood.

DAVID MALOUF

South Of My Days

South of my days' circle, part of my blood's country,
rises that tableland, high delicate outline
of bony slopes wincing under the winter,
low trees blue-leaved and olive, outcropping granite—
clean, lean, hungry country. The creek's leaf-silenced,
willow-choked, the slope a tangle of medlar and crabapple
branching over and under, blotched with a green lichen;
and the old cottage lurches in for shelter.

O cold the black-frost night. The walls draw in to the warmth
and the old roof cracks its joints; the slung kettle
hisses a leak on the fire. Hardly to be believed that summer
will turn up again some day in a wave of rambler roses,
thrust its hot face in here to tell another yarn—
a story old Dan can spin into a blanket against the winter.
Seventy years of stories he clutches round his bones.
Seventy summers are hived in him like old honey.

Droving that year, Charleville to the Hunter,
nineteen-one it was, and the drought beginning;
sixty head left at the McIntyre, the mud round them
hardened like iron; and the yellow boy died
in the sulky ahead with the gear, but the horse went on,
stopped at the Sandy Camp and waited in the evening.
It was the flies we seen first, swarming like bees.
Came to the Hunter, three hundred head of a thousand—
cruel to keep them alive—and the river was dust.

Or mustering up in the Bogongs in the autumn
when the blizzards came early. Brought them down; we brought them
down, what aren't there yet. Or driving for Cobb's on the run
up from Tamworth—Thunderbolt at the top of Hungry Hill,
and I give him a wink. I wouldn't wait long, Fred,
not if I was you; the troopers are just behind,
coming for that job at the Hillgrove. He went like a luny,
him on his big black horse.
                    Oh, they slide and they vanish
as he shuffles the years like a pack of conjuror's cards.
True or not, it's all the same; and the frost on the roof
cracks like a whip, and the back-log breaks into ash.
Wake, old man. This is winter, and the yarns are over.
No one is listening.
                    South of my days' circle
I know it dark against the stars, the high lean country
full of old stories that still go walking in my sleep.

JUDITH WRIGHT

Performance

ave you ever been to a poetry reading? The impact of a poem can be increased tenfold hearing it delivered with clarity, understanding and the appropriate feeling. See if there are any recordings in your school library of poets reading their own work, and make time to listen to them.

In this chapter, in pairs and in groups, *you* will be taking poetry from simple effective readings to the peaks of performance—drawing on choral effects, visual images, music and other sound effects to present moving and dramatic production numbers!

The power to persuade

ACTIVITY

The following poems deal directly or indirectly with an issue of concern to us all. This activity will help to highlight their respective themes or messages.

1 Make pairs and choose one of the poems or sets of poems. Together, explore the ideas and issues raised in the poem.

2 The task of one student is to prepare and rehearse for a reading of the poem.

3 The other student is to prepare a brief (say, one or two minute) emotive persuasive speech on the issue. The aim of the speech is to stir your peers to think about the issues the poet has raised. Carefully choose each word and phrase of your speech to stir, to move, to impress. It may help to imagine that you have only one or two

precious minutes to speak to a potentially influential group on an issue or cause that you feel very strongly about.

4 Each pair presents their reading and speech to the class 'audience', who will jot down notes or questions for a general discussion when all the performances have been presented.

In the New Landscape

In the new landscape there will be only cars
and drivers of cars and signs saying
FREE SWAP CARDS HERE
and exhaust-fumes drifting over the countryside
and sounds of acceleration instead of birdsong

In the new landscape there will be no more streets
begging for hopscotch squares, only roads
the full width between buildings and a packed mob
of hoods surging between stop-lights
—so dense a sheep-dog with asbestos pads
could safely trot across
(Streets will be underground and pedestrians pale.
Motorists on the other hand will be tanned.)

In the new landscape there will be no trees
unless as exotica for parking lots
—and weeds,
weeds, too, will be no more

And we will construct in keeping with these times
a concrete god with streamlined attributes
not likely to go soft at the sight or sound of
little children under the front wheels
or lovers who have wilfully forgotten
to keep their eyes on the road,
while by a ceremonial honking of motor-horns
we'll raise a daily anthem of praise
to him in whose stone lap are laid
the morning sacrifices, freshly-garlanded, death's
        rictus carved
on each face with the sharp obsidian blade
of fortuitousness (steam-hoses will be used
to cleanse the altar . . .)

And in the new landscape after a century or so
of costly research it will be found
that even the irreplaceable parts
will be replaceable, after which
there will be only cars

                                    BRUCE DAWE

I Followed a Butterfly

In a mountain of meadows I followed a butterfly,
        a creation of colour,
in a meadow of maps I followed stinking city streets
        and ageing alleys,
in a map of landscape I followed nature's will and
        vivid vigour,
and in a landscape of parking lots and pleasure-seeking
        places, I turned away.

JUDY SHRIMPTON
(STUDENT)

In the Forest

Wait for the axe sound in the forest.
The birds wait. The lizards pause
and wait. The creatures that are nearest
earth feel the approaching pace

measure a man. And they must wait.
Then has the time come? The dark
of forest is so solid that
its inter-growth should never break.

But has the time come? The birds
are nervous, see them flinch and turn.
The snake moves into the reeds
quickly. Danger, the signs warn.

That! Slap of an axe. That!
There, quick, over there. The tree
is tensed. In its green height
the possums clutch their young; they flee.

Crack again crack of slow man's weapon,
intolerable wait for the one tree's sake
for its grasping fall and its death to happen
and the gash in the forest, and light to break.

Now, says the axe, and the tree is fallen,
the spider crushed in its secret nest.
The late slow lives have been taken,
in the sheltering tree they have been crushed.

The accepted world is quickly broken,
the skull of the forest is opened up.
Now, means the axe. But the birds have forgotten—
there are other trees; they prepare for sleep.

THOMAS SHAPCOTT

In My World

In my world
I would write
of golden suns
if it weren't
for the obscuring clouds.
I would write
of the wind-bent grass
but all the fields
are tarmacked
& multistorey.
Instead I'll be
an urban Wordsworth
writing of
reinforced concrete landscapes
& clearbrown skies
where
to wander lonely as a cloud
is just not advisable
after dark.

STEVE TURNER

Why?

White bodies and dark
    gravitating towards
        a solar source of beat

and rhythm
    Pulsating as one
        body of movement
            bound by their love of music

we see them
    What is the reason
        people of slums
            regardless of race, religion,

pigmentation
    Dance their undulated
        rhythmic dances
            born with the gift of music

appreciation
    Whereas politicians
        with money, identity
            must argue, question and

debate
    The eternal racism
        conflict, unknown to
            them their own minds

create?

ANITA PITCHER
(STUDENT)

The Zulu Girl

When in the sun the hot red acres smoulder,
Down where the sweating gang its labour plies,
A girl flings down her hoe, and from her shoulder
Unslings her child tormented by the flies.

She takes him to a ring of shadow pooled
By thorn-trees: purpled with the blood of ticks,
While her sharp nails, in slow caresses ruled,
Prowl through his hair with sharp electric clicks.

His sleepy mouth, plugged by the heavy nipple,
Tugs like a puppy, grunting as he feeds:
Through his frail nerves her own deep languors ripple
Like a broad river sighing through its reeds.

Yet in that drowsy stream his flesh imbibes
An old unquenched unsmotherable heat—
The curbed ferocity of beaten tribes,
The sullen dignity of their defeat.

Her body looms above him like a hill
Within whose shade a village lies at rest,
Or the first cloud so terrible and still
That bears the coming harvest in its breast.

ROY CAMPBELL

Petition

At Hiroshima
A hundred thousand people were being
Good and bad and all the mixtures that are people:
Then someone dropped a bomb
And the whole hundred thousand
Stopped being.
Some hundreds survived:
The mutilations are on view in several hospitals
And two-headed progeny may be expected.
That was some years ago
And in Japan.
I wasn't responsible.
I signed a petition once,
Asking I know not who
That the bomb happen again nowhere ever.
Today my Gwen and five hundred thousand others
Are being good and bad and all the mixtures that are people
In Brisbane.
I hope someone read my petition.

R. G. HAY

Prosperity

monday to friday at the plant
concrete yards are busy with
vehicles and movement altho most of what
moves is machinery
now and then a human figure crosses the open
space looking small & helpless
in the sky above the plant not much is blue
behind the buildings in a grey channel something
oozes past seeming to have been a river

on friday night when the machines are silent
& the watchman finishes his rounds
walking away with gun and torch like some
mistaken supplicant then only the dark
finds its way through wire fences
and sometimes due to atmospheric conditions (for which
the management is not responsible) the wind will rise
or in the wasteland hours of industrial sunday
rain might start falling inadvertently as if
still thinking of a plant as some kind of
flower

MICHAEL DRANSFIELD

No Speech from the Scaffold

There will be no speech from
the scaffold, the scene must
be its own commentary.

The glossy chipped
surface of the block is like
something for kitchen use.

And the masked man with his
chopper: we know him: he
works in a warehouse nearby.

Last, the prisoner, he
is pale, he walks through
the dewy grass, nodding

a goodbye to acquaintances.
There will be no speech. And we
have forgotten his offence.

What he did is, now,
immaterial. It is the
execution that matters, or,

rather, it is his conduct
as he rests there, while
he is still a human.

THOM GUNN

Mood and feeling

1 In pairs, read through the following poems. Each has been chosen because it evokes a certain mood or feeling.

2 Choose one of the poems for closer study and discussion together. Look closely at the *language* used and the *rhythm* or *movement* of the lines.
   - What mood has the poet created through choice of words and manipulation of rhythm or movement of the lines?
   - What feelings does the poem arouse in you, the reader?

3 Your task now is to 'produce' the poem in such a way that its mood and feeling are accentuated. It is suggested that:
   a One of you reads and rehearses the poem until you feel you have vocally captured and relayed the mood and could arouse the feelings in your audience the poet intended. Pay special attention in your reading to:
      - punctuation and pause
      - metre (if relevant)
      - the 'colour' and suggestion of particular words and phrases
      - rhyme that is intended as emphasis
      - alliteration, assonance or consonance that helps suggest, emphasize or exaggerate
      - particularly evocative images
      - repetition that reinforces an idea, a feeling, a mood.

   b The other chooses appropriate background music and/or sound effects to accompany the reading which will similarly reflect the poem's mood and arouse the appropriate feelings.

   It is best to work together on both tasks—suggesting, helping, testing, rehearsing.

4 Present your production to the rest of the class.

Break, Break, Break

Break, break, break,
   On thy cold grey stones, O Sea!
And I would that my tongue could utter
   The thoughts that arise in me.

O well for the fisherman's boy
   That he shouts with his sister at play!
O well for the sailor lad,
   That he sings in his boat on the bay!

And the stately ships go on
   To their haven under the hill;
For O for the touch of a vanished hand,
   And the sound of a voice that is still!

Break, break, break,
    At the foot of thy crags, O Sea!
But the tender grace of a day that is dead
    Will never come back to me.

ALFRED, LORD TENNYSON

The Company of Lovers

We meet and part now over all the world,
        We, the lost company,
take hands together in the night, forget
the night in our brief happiness, silently.
We who sought many things, throw all away
for this one thing, one only,
remembering that in the narrow grave
we shall be lonely.

Death marshals up his armies round us now.
Their footsteps crowd too near.
Lock your warm hand above the chilling heart
and for a time I live without my fear.
Grope in the night to find me and embrace,
for the dark preludes of the drums begin,
and round us, round the company of lovers,
Death draws his cordons in.

JUDITH WRIGHT

Taylor Street

The small porch of imitation
marble is never sunny, but
outside the front door he
sits on his kitchen chair facing
the street. In the bent yellowish
face, from under the brim
of a floppy brown hat,
his small eyes watch what
he is not living. But he
lives what he can:
watches without a smile, with
a certain strain, the warmth
of his big crumpled
body anxiously cupped
by himself in himself, as
he leans over himself not
over the cold railing, un-
moving but carefully getting
a little strength from the sight of the
passers-by. He has it
all planned: he will live
here morning by morning.

THOM GUNN

Forgotten Dreamtime

Eucalypt corroboree, rise to meet the sun,
The children of the dreamtime are long since gone,
Mourn for their passing, for they have
    turned to stone,
And eucalyptus must corroboree all by its own.

Kangaroo, wallaby,
Hunters chase and follow thee,
Boomerang enchantment, they disappear, all gone,
Hunter chased by white spirits from ancestral home.

Koala, wombat,
We steal it back by lies,
Throw the spear at White Devils
And run for our lives.

Eucalypt corroboree, rise to meet the sun,
The little people, the hunters, have long since gone.
Mourn for the warriors, they no longer dance
And Eucalyptus must didgeridoo in its rigid stance.

NADIA HARMSEN
(STUDENT)

Daily London Recipe

Take any number of them
you can think of.
pour into empty red bus
    until full.
and then push in
    ten more.
Allow enough time
to get hot under the collar
before transferring into
multistorey building.
Leave for eight hours,
and pour back into same bus
    already half full
    Scrape remainder off.
When settled down
tip into terraced houses each
carefully lined with copy of
The Standard and *Tit Bits*.
Place mixture before open
television screen at 7 p.m.
and then allow to cool
in bed at 10.30 p.m.
May be served with
working overalls
or pinstripe suit

STEVE TURNER

Pied Beauty

Glory be to God for dappled things—
    For skies of couple-colour as a brinded cow;
      For rose-moles all in stipple upon trout that swim;
Fresh-firecoal chestnut-falls; finches' wings;
    Landscape plotted and pieced—fold, fallow, and plough;
      And all trades, their gear and tackle and trim.

All things counter, original, spare, strange;
    Whatever is fickle, freckled (who knows how?)
      With swift, slow; sweet, sour; adazzle, dim;
He fathers-forth whose beauty is past change:
    Praise him.

GERARD MANLEY HOPKINS

Individual interpretation

3
ACTIVITY

Reading a poem aloud is a matter of vocally interpreting the language and devices the poet has used. It is not a great deal different from reading music—we must interpret the shades of sound; the changes in tone, mood, pace and rhythm; pauses; the stressed and unstressed words, phrases and images.

1 Choose a poem from the selection following on pages 93–96 and explore it in terms of the following:

Tone/mood/feeling
• What is the overall tone of the poem?
• Does it vary at all?
• Can you reflect this tone/mood and its variations with your voice?

Rhythm/movement
• Is there an obvious rhythmic pattern?
• Does the *sense* of certain lines or phrases indicate a certain pace?

Pauses
• Commas, semi-colons, full-stops and dashes will need to be given their appropriate pause value.
• Be sensitive to obvious lack of pause, for example run-on lines and verses and unpunctuated listing.

Rhyme
• Does the poet use rhyme (internal or external) to stress or emphasize words or ideas?

Assonance/alliteration
• These devices usually highlight and enrich the sound of certain words and the links between them. They can also help establish a certain mood and pace. Consider how heavily you should emphasize them.

2 With these criteria to guide you, write *oral interpretation notes* for the poem you have chosen to present. (All the poems in the selection provide the opportunity to fulfill all the criteria.) Here is a model:

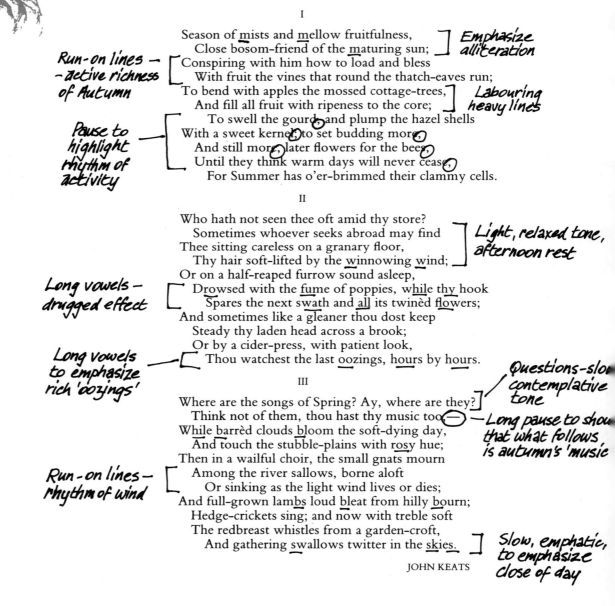

Ode to Autumn

I

Season of mists and mellow fruitfulness,
   Close bosom-friend of the maturing sun;
Conspiring with him how to load and bless
   With fruit the vines that round the thatch-eaves run;
To bend with apples the mossed cottage-trees,
   And fill all fruit with ripeness to the core;
      To swell the gourd, and plump the hazel shells
With a sweet kernel; to set budding more,
   And still more, later flowers for the bees,
   Until they think warm days will never cease,
      For Summer has o'er-brimmed their clammy cells.

Run-on lines — — active richness of Autumn

Emphasize alliteration

Labouring heavy lines

Pause to highlight rhythm of activity

II

Who hath not seen thee oft amid thy store?
   Sometimes whoever seeks abroad may find
Thee sitting careless on a granary floor,
   Thy hair soft-lifted by the winnowing wind;
Or on a half-reaped furrow sound asleep,
   Drowsed with the fume of poppies, while thy hook
      Spares the next swath and all its twinèd flowers;
And sometimes like a gleaner thou dost keep
   Steady thy laden head across a brook;
   Or by a cider-press, with patient look,
      Thou watchest the last oozings, hours by hours.

Light, relaxed tone, afternoon rest

Long vowels — drugged effect

Long vowels to emphasize rich 'oozings'

III

Where are the songs of Spring? Ay, where are they?
   Think not of them, thou hast thy music too,—
While barrèd clouds bloom the soft-dying day,
   And touch the stubble-plains with rosy hue;
Then in a wailful choir, the small gnats mourn
   Among the river sallows, borne aloft
      Or sinking as the light wind lives or dies;
And full-grown lambs loud bleat from hilly bourn;
   Hedge-crickets sing; and now with treble soft
   The redbreast whistles from a garden-croft,
      And gathering swallows twitter in the skies.

                                        JOHN KEATS

Questions—slow contemplative tone

Long pause to show that what follows is autumn's 'music'

Run-on lines — rhythm of wind

Slow, emphatic, to emphasize close of day

3 Practise reading the poem until you feel you have done justice to it.
Recording your efforts for critical listening can be a big help here.

4 Present your poem to the class, either on tape or in person.
The class 'audience' could perhaps evaluate your performance, based
on your use of the five criteria listed earlier.

A Night Of Rain

A night of rain and the trains pulling out,
like centipedes, joint by joint crawling north,
south, west, eyes pair by pair peering out
on a night of rain. A night of danger
hissed along highways, the wipers erasing
a serial vision of unachievable terminal;
the radios burbling I gotta go static I gotta
go travelling on I've played and laid around
in this old town too long. The sound
is for everyone, on the grave of my father
and on my grandfather and on
the angel going over my own.
                  And on the battlefields
defeat say the unstressed feet of the rain
rhythmless, raggedly drumming out
to no retreat, no parley. The slain go foot by foot
both over and under the ground on a night of rain.
                  When I was a child
my grandfather gave me a book
on Moths. Copy them perfectly he said.
He went over his vines with scissors
snipping the grubs in two. They bled
their greenish-white insides.
Another night I was sick
his rough hand on my damp head
crooned. A night of rain and danger.
The wipers copy me perfectly,
this-way-and-that wings rubbering out
a serial vision of round the bend is Not.

ANNE ELDER

Drought

She will not forgive the sun's
malicious fingers,
prying day open
through curtainless cracks.
Wearied by sleep
that trickles rest,
her shrunken body drags.
With turgid arms
she wrings their thin milk
from the cows.

Drought hangs granular over the farm,
dusting itself through the dying trees,
scratching the house,
             her asperous skin.
She smells its flatness.
Nothing moves.
Even the gnarl of gums
is straight and grey with heat.
The wattle has long crushed
its maizey buds into the dirt
pleading for damp;
and the juice-less grass
is lost in the papery earth.

The only sound
is the endless crank of hours.
Her greenness is boarded up
like the cool darkness of an old shack;
tightly she is gripped
in the bone-whiteness of the day.

                    ROBYN ROWLAND

Train Journey

Glassed with cold sleep and dazzled by the moon,
out of the confused hammering dark of the train
I looked and saw under the moon's cold sheet
your delicate dry breasts, country that built my heart;

and the small trees on their uncoloured slope
like poetry moved, articulate and sharp
and purposeful under the great dry flight of air,
under the crosswise currents of wind and star.

Clench down your strength, box-tree and ironbark.
Break with your violent root the virgin rock.
Draw from the flying dark its breath of dew
till the unliving come to life in you.

Be over the blind rock a skin of sense,
under the barren height a slender dance.
I woke and saw the dark small trees that burn
suddenly into flowers more lovely than the white moon.

                    JUDITH WRIGHT

Death, Be Not Proud

Death, be not proud, though some have callèd thee
Mighty and dreadful, for thou art not so:
For those, whom thou think'st thou dost overthrow,
Die not, poor Death; nor yet canst thou kill me.
From rest and sleep, which but thy picture be,

Much pleasure, then from thee much more must flow;
And soonest our best men with thee do go—
Rest of their bones and souls' delivery!
Thou'rt slave to Fate, chance, kings, and desperate men,
And dost with poison, war, and sickness dwell;
And poppy or charms can make us sleep as well
And better than thy stroke. Why swell'st thou then?
One short sleep past, we wake eternally,
And Death shall be no more: Death, thou shalt die!

JOHN DONNE

Drought

Midsummer noon; and the timbered walls
start in the heat,
and the children sag listlessly over the desks,
with bloodless faces oozing sweat
sipped by the stinging flies.
Outside, the tall sun fades the shabby mallee
and drives the ants deep underground;
the stony driftsand shrivels
the drab, sparse plants;
there's not a cloud in all the sky to cast
a shadow on the tremulous plain.
Stirless the windmills: thirsty cattle standing
despondently about the empty tanks,
stamping and tossing their heads
in torment of the flies from dawn to dark.

For ten parched days it has been like this,
and, although I love the desert, I
have found myself
                    dreaming
of upright gums by a mountain creek
where the red boronia blooms,
where bellbirds chime through the morning mists,
and greenness can hide from the sun;
of rock-holes where the brumbies slink
like swift cloud shadows from the gidgi scrub
to drink when the moon is low.

    And as I stoop to drink, I too,
just as I raise my cupped hands to my lips,
I am recalled to this drought-stricken plain
by the petulant question
of a summer-wearied child.

FLEXMORE HUDSON

Spring

Nothing is so beautiful as spring—
    When weeds, in wheels, shoot long and lovely and lush;
    Thrush's eggs look little low heavens, and thrush
Through the echoing timber does so rinse and wring
The ear, it strikes like lightnings to hear him sing;
    The glassy peartree leaves and blooms, they brush
    The descending blue; that blue is all in a rush
With richness; the racing lambs too have fair their fling.

What is all this juice and all this joy?
    A strain of the earth's sweet being in the beginning
In Eden garden.—Have, get, before it cloy,
    Before it cloud, Christ, lord, and sour with sinning,
Innocent mind and Mayday in girl and boy,
    Most, O maid's child, thy choice and worthy the winning.

                                                GERARD MANLEY HOPKINS

4 ACTIVITY

Variations on voice

Your task is to use a small group of four to six *voices* to orally produce a poem.

1 Choose one of the following poems and in your group come to an understanding of its content and purpose.

2 Discuss ways in which your group might orally recite the poem. Here are some possibilities:
   • a straight choral reading
   • a blend of individual and choral reading
   • use of single voices to emphasize tone or intention
   • varied use of individual voices only
   • the echoing or repetition of appropriate lines
   • a blend of orator and audience (minister and congregation, for example).

   Add whatever voice effects you consider appropriate, for example murmuring in the background, humming, sounds of joy, misery, approval, etc.

3 Prepare and rehearse your production. There are many other possibilities besides those listed above. Use your voices in *whatever* way you think will help to capture and re-create the poem's tone, feeling and intention.

4 Each group now performs its work for the whole class. Perhaps a panel of judges could be appointed to award first, second, and third places and to justify their choice in a brief address to the class.

The Young Dead Soldiers
To Richard Myers

The young dead soldiers do not speak.
Nevertheless they are heard in the still houses.
(Who has not heard them?)

They have a silence that speaks for them at night
And when the clock counts.

They say,
We were young. We have died. Remember us.

They say,
We have done what we could
But until it is finished it is not done.

They say,
We have given our lives
But until it is finished no one can know what our
        lives gave.

They say,
Our deaths are not ours,
They are yours,
They will mean what you make them.

They say,
Whether our lives and our deaths were for peace
        and a new hope
Or for nothing
We cannot say,
It is you who must say this.

They say,
We leave you our deaths,
Give them their meaning,
Give them an end to the war and a true peace,
Give them a victory that ends the war and a peace afterwards
Give them their meaning.

We were young, they say.
We have died.
Remember us.

ARCHIBALD MACLEISH

Brother and Sisters

The road turned out to be a cul-de-sac;
stopped like a lost intention at the gate
and never crossed the mountains to the coast.
But they stayed on. Years grew like grass and leaves

across the half-erased and dubious track
until one day they knew the plans were lost,
the blue-print for the bridge was out of date,
and now their orchards never would be planted.
The saplings sprouted slyly; day by day

the bush moved one step nearer, wondering when.
The polished parlour grew distrait and haunted
where Millie, Lucy, John each night at ten
wound the gilt clock that leaked the year away.

The pianola—oh, listen to the mocking-bird—
wavers on Sundays and has lost a note.
The wrinkled ewes snatch pansies through the fence
and stare with shallow eyes into the garden
where Lucy shrivels waiting for a word,
and Millie's cameos loosen round her throat.
The bush comes near, the ranges grow immense.

Feeding the lambs deserted in early spring
Lucy looked up and saw the stockman's eye
telling her she was cracked and old.
                                    The wall
groans in the night and settles more awry.
O how they lie awake. Their thoughts go fluttering
from room to room like moths: 'Millie, are you awake?'
'Oh John. I have been dreaming.' 'Lucy, do you cry?'
—meet tentative as moths. Antennae stroke a wing.
'There is nothing to be afraid of. Nothing at all.'

JUDITH WRIGHT

Suburban Lullaby

Fear the lights that cross the street,
Fear the blackout shadows grim,
Fear the bobby on his beat,
Fear the one that watches him:
    Fear the shock when they collide;
    Hurry, hurry home and hide.

Fear the lifting of the bolt;
Fear the fingers at the door:
Friendly hands may thumb a Colt,
Friendly things are friends no more.
    Voices crack that cry, "All's well."
    Creep to bed and dream of hell.

History naked rides the sky;
Can you take him by the mane?
Is there time to justify?
Is there time to start again?
    Dare to hold or dare let go,
    What abysses gape below!

JOHN MANIFOLD

Open Invitation, Or
You Too Can Have a Body Politic Like Ours
If You're Not Careful!

Come unto me all ye who protest and are pamphlet-laden
and I will get you arrested why now
we can *all* be communists! No longer
is it necessary to read Marx and inwardly digest
—you too can be a communist-radical-dupe
by courtesy of the Traffic Act of 1949 . . . Simplicity
itself! No more night-study of *Das Kapital*
and *On Guerilla Warfare* by their thongs
ye shall know them (not to mention their
ANTI-URANIUM T-shirts!) so don't think you can come here
hot from your Kremlin-sponsored pot-shops
and fill this lawful orderly Palatinate
with articles of dissent we know
your type from way back crawling
from the ubiquitous tertiary slime and the jungles of the Far North
and corrupted South into the light of our tourist-oriented
primeval day *Back back you monsters the Jurassic*
is 500 million years ahead Charles Darwin
you have just been given
a lawful direction and a thousand anti-evolutionists in the columns
                                        of provincial newspapers
can't be wrong and as for you Herr Luther
your Ninety-five Theses on that church-door at Wittenburg
are in clear violation of the regulation requiring placards to be
no more than 610 square millimetres *and of cardboard* and I must
                                                        warn you
that if you step off any city footpath objecting to
the selling of indulgences or yellow-cake
you will have graduated as fully-qualified
SCUM to appear in court on Monday morning
charged with whatever we can think up in the meantime
So take your pick mate, either a quick thump in the ear a night in the
                        cells a fifty-dollar fine
                        and the democratic right to dissent
or a quiet night at home with the wife and kids and
                        watch it all happening to Thomas More
                        and Galileo in Sanyo-Colour
                        on the Six-O'Clock News—the choice
(as always in a democracy)
is YOURS!

BRUCE DAWE

The Tyger

Tyger! Tyger! burning bright
In the forests of the night,
What immortal hand or eye
Could frame thy fearful symmetry?

In what distant deeps or skies
Burnt the fire of thine eyes?
On what wings dare he aspire?
What the hand dare seize the fire?

And what shoulder, and what art,
Could twist the sinews of thy heart?
And when thy heart began to beat,
What dread hand? and what dread feet?

What the hammer? what the chain?
In what furnace was thy brain?
What the anvil? what dread grasp
Dare its deadly terror clasp?

When the stars threw down their spears,
And watered heaven with their tears,
Did he smile his work to see?
Did he who made the Lamb make thee?

Tyger! Tyger! burning bright
In the forests of the night,
What immortal hand or eye
Dare frame thy fearful symmetry?

WILLIAM BLAKE

Evening

1

Night slowly expands across the city; a full moon appears, a white
counter.

In the suburbs it is dusty as torchlight, there are houses on stilts,
houses brown and heavy as pennies with the face of the
dead Queen.

And in the sky stormclouds gather, the evening's headache.

In the houses there are dolls with bright fixed eyes kept under beds
with broken clocks and women's hats with orchids,
dangling fruit.
In shop windows the dead are assembling, dressed in all the fashions
of the living.

We try to fathom their faces, squeezing ourselves against the glass,
bequeathing them our breath.

And everywhere this darkness, as in the corners of Cathedrals.

A breeze brings the smell of rotting cardboard from the docks, and
smoke from the last ferry casting off, about to cross the
black river.

A boy stands on board with his father; he looks into the sky and
sees the moon, he looks into the waters: the moon is there
also.

2

On Ann Street and Elizabeth Street, on the dead-end roads, and all
    down the river that glitters like a snail's trail,
    the full moon shines.

All night she wanders the streets, with nothing to do, she looks into
    our windows and sees cane furniture like
    stick-insects, a cat lapping milk in a dark kitchen.

She lingers on Roma Street Station, smelling old leather suitcases.

She peers into verandahs and bedrooms, examining the whites of
    eyes, of those who cannot sleep, who pour themselves
    another drink. She cools their glasses.

She is with the ship coming towards the harbour, with those who
    can only just see the city, a string of lights, a rosary.

On the hospitals and churches, on the bamboo that knots in
    overgrown gardens, she shines, accepting everything.

Those still out this night look up; the moon is in the highest point of
    the sky, above each one of them.

She settles on tables and changes them to altars, she sits at the
    bottom of puddles,

While over all the city a steady rain begins to fall, the sound of
    many clocks.

KEVIN HART

Group productions

An interesting way to come to an understanding of a poem is to explore
the different ways in which it can be re-created, illustrated or produced
in other media—print, sound, stage or screen, or a combination of any
of these.

First, however, it is necessary to find clues as to the poet's intention
or message so that this can be made obvious in the production. These
clues can be found in the poem's *tone*, *rhyme*, *rhythm*, *language* and
imagery, and in any of the other poetic 'tools' we have explored.

As an example, read Vincent Buckley's poem *Election Speech* and the
sample production notes which follow it.

Election Speech

Mottoes: words blown through a skull,
Programmes unwinding like a chain.
We listen, prurient and dull,
Each one bound by fear or gain
To the last ranting syllable.

Invented perils bring the sweat
Onto his practised lip. No doubt,

However, we shall live to eat
The meals that spin tomorrow out,
No doubt we'll lie in comfort yet

And drive each other to the polls.
Present and future weigh on us
Not as this glib voice recalls
But like a headless incubus,
Deaths, terrors that no vote controls.

He goes in quickly for the kill:
A fact, a promise, and a jibe.
I think of nothing; nothings fill
The image that his words inscribe,
My skull intoning from the hill.

VINCENT BUCKLEY

Production notes for *Election Speech*
Stage 1—message

Rhythm and rhyme	• very regular—monotonous? hollow effect? • rhyme emphasizes words like 'skull', 'dull'; 'polls', 'controls'.
Tone	• tone of bored detachment created by above • cynical view of politicians emphasized by language: 'glib voice', 'ranting', 'invented perils', 'practised lips'.
Language and imagery	• in addition to above, phrases like: • 'words blown through a skull' (in one ear and out the other) • 'unwinding like a chain' (never ending, boring) • 'prurient and dull' • 'drive each other to the polls'.

Overall, the message seems to be that the pointless, often dishonest prattling of politicians does little to inspire us and little to positively affect the lives we lead.

Stage 2—production possibilities

Print	• political slogans, posters, headlines; electioneering photographs, stickers, pamphlets • other? cartoons, artwork, effigy?
Sound	• read poem over recording of a parliamentary session or election speech • student-written electioneering satire as fill-in or in background • chanting of political slogans as poem is being read—maybe satirized? • other? interviews, music, sound effects?
Stage	• mime of voters (mechanical, mindless movements) at polling booths; mime of politicians

- props to demonstrate 'paper warfare'
- 'before and after' scenes of political conduct
- other? freeze frames? dramatization of whole poem?

Screen
- video clips of above (or similar)
- video clips of politicians speaking, remonstrating (without sound to demonstrate hollowness of their words?)
- other? slide/tape presentations?

ACTIVITY

Each of the following poems are suitable for a group production.

1 Make a group of about four and choose one poem for a produced performance.

2 Draw up production notes for both stages of the process (as illustrated). Remember, not all media need be used; you may choose any or a combination of the print, sound, stage and screen possibilities.

3 Create and draw together your chosen media.

4 Rehearse your production and present it to the rest of the class.

The News And Weather

A man shot a man who shot a man who shot a man
Said it wasn't murder it just went off in his hand
We got a bigger bomb than the one we had before
On the Middle East border there wasn't any score
Some people starved to death in a city far away
A man in a suit will read the weather for today
A man in a suit will read the weather for today

A spokesman said he could not comment at the time
A friend of a friend said the rumour was a lie
The next door neighbour always thought that he was funny
The man who guessed the draw was given lots of money
The corrupt M.P. said he'd nothing more to say
A man in a suit will read the weather for today
A man in a suit will read the weather for today

The star of thirty films has just cast his fifth wife
The man who killed children must stay indoors for life
The financial index is falling down again
Pence to the dollar to the mark to the yen
Tobaccco and petrol and the price you'll have to pay
A man in a suit will read the weather for today
A man in a suit will read the weather for today

At the football match it was the crowd who went and lost
The team managers are trying to estimate the cost
The little girl went missing only three days ago
Don't travel by train because they're on a go-slow
A leading tennis player has admitted that he's gay
A man in a suit will read the weather for today
A man in a suit will read the weather for today

Policemen say watch out for strangers at your door
Ring this number if you've seen this man before
Another soldier died but he didn't have a girl
There's been a great disaster the biggest in the world
Yet down at the zoo the woolly bears come out to play
A man in a suit will read the weather for today
A man in a suit will read the weather for today

A two minute warning will follow this newscast
You'll hear a high pitched noise, then you'll hear a blast
The windows will go missing, you'll be blinded by a light
But if you remain calm everything will be alright
Some of you may notice that your skin will peel away
A man in a suit will read the weather for today
A man in a suit will read the weather for today.

STEVE TURNER

This Is Your Death

This is your death
When sunlight breathes on the wall
And you draw the curtain;
When you turn from the ruby-gleam fairground and say,
"Not for me".

This is your death
When the News reports Christ's crucifixion
You lean back and suck your pipe;
When you choose for your nephew's birthday
A miniature megaton rocket.

This is your death
When they lynch a nigger and you answer,
"Progress takes time";
When the tin can drags down the cat's tail
But you cross the road.

This is your death
When the bomber bolts are screwed by your spanner
And you say, "It's only a job";
Or having glimpsed a streak of the morning
You decay into fame.

This is your death
When you state. "I am not me
But two or three people:
A skilled professional slayer
And a kind father".

This your death
When millions are dying you respond,
"It's up to the others";
When you say, "Life is good"
Yet won't live it —
This, this is your death.

PAT ARROWSMITH

A Litany

For those who grasp their prison bars helplessly that we may walk free —
    a thought.
For those who rot in the dark so that we may walk in the sun —
    a thought.
For those whose ribs have been broken so that we may breathe our fill —
    a thought.
For those whose back has been broken so that we may walk erect —
    a thought.
For those whose faces have been slapped so that we may walk in fear of no
hand —
    a thought.
For those whose mouths have been gagged so that we may speak out —
    a thought.
For those whose pride lies in rags on the slabs of their jails so that we may
proudly walk —
    a thought.
For those whose wives live in anguish so that our wives may live happily —
    a thought.
For those whose country is in chains so that our country may be free —
    a thought.
And for their jailers and for their torturers —
    a thought.
The saddest of all, they are the most maimed,
and the Day of reckoning is bound to come.

SALVADOR DE MADARIAGA

God's Grandeur

The world is charged with the grandeur of God.
  It will flame out, like shining from shook foil;
  It gathers to a greatness, like the ooze of oil
Crushed. Why do men then now not reck his rod?
Generations have trod, have trod, have trod;
  And all is seared with trade; bleared, smeared with toil;
  And wears man's smudge and shares man's smell: the soil
Is bare now, nor can foot feel, being shod.

And for all this, nature is never spent;
  There lives the dearest freshness deep down things;
And though the last lights off the black West went
  Oh, morning, at the brown brink eastward, springs—
Because the Holy Ghost over the bent
  World broods with warm breast and with ah! bright wings.

GERARD MANLEY HOPKINS

Preludes

I

The winter evening settles down
With smell of steaks in passageways.
Six o'clock.
The burnt-out ends of smoky days.
And now a gusty shower wraps
The grimy scraps
Of withered leaves about your feet
And newspapers from vacant lots;
The showers beat
On broken blinds and chimney-pots,
And at the corner of the street
A lonely cab-horse steams and stamps.

And then the lighting of the lamps.

II

The morning comes to consciousness
Of faint stale smells of beer
From the sawdust-trampled street
With all its muddy feet that press
To early coffee-stands.

With the other masquerades
That time resumes,
One thinks of all the hands
That are raising dingy shades
In a thousand furnished rooms.

III

You tossed a blanket from the bed,
You lay upon your back, and waited;
You dozed, and watched the night revealing
The thousand sordid images
Of which your soul was constituted;
They flickered against the ceiling.
And when all the world came back
And the light crept up between the shutters
And you heard the sparrows in the gutters,
You had such a vision of the street
As the street hardly understands;
Sitting along the bed's edge, where
You curled the papers from your hair,
Or clasped the yellow soles of feet
In the palms of both soiled hands.

IV

His soul stretched tight across the skies
That fade behind a city block.
Or trampled by insistent feet
At four and five and six o'clock;
And short square fingers stuffing pipes,
And evening newspapers, and eyes
Assured of certain certainties,
The conscience of a blackened street
Impatient to assume the world.

I am moved by fancies that are curled
Around these images, and cling:
The notion of some infinitely gentle
Infinitely suffering thing.

Wipe your hands across your mouth, and laugh;
The worlds revolve like ancient women
Gathering fuel in vacant lots.

T. S. ELIOT

7
Modelling

ACTIVITY

*M*odelling—using another poem as a model for your own—is an excellent way of getting started in your own poetry composition, especially if you are not easily inspired.

Fantasy

The following poems may inspire you to think creatively about your future and to pen your wildest dreams.

Points to model:
- a creative emphasis on the outlandish, the weird and wonderful
- the bringing together of very different items
- the witty conclusions

A Boy's Head

In it there is a space-ship
and a project
for doing away with piano lessons.

And there is
Noah's ark,
which shall be first.

And there is
an entirely new bird,
an entirely new hare,
an entirely new bumble-bee.

There is a river
that flows upwards.

There is a multiplication table.

There is anti–matter.

And it just cannot be trimmed.

I believe
that only what cannot be trimmed
is a head

There is much promise
in the circumstance
that so many people have heads.

MIROSLAV HOLUB

My Friend's Head

In it there is a romance story,
Screams, plots and double plots,
A liquidizer full of younger brother.

In it there's a Jekyll and Hyde,
An assassination attempt on the next-
door neighbour,
To stop him singing in the bath.
There's a triangular prism,
Turning slowly,
Soft pink shapes,
Giant marshmallows,
A sandy beach,
A Sherman tank,
An acid bath full of teachers.

KATY SENIOR
(STUDENT)

Look over what you have written and ask yourself whether you think your description is as striking and as original as you can make it.

Try putting your lines in a different order, adding one or two different images and ideas.

Cut out the parts that seem less satisfactory even if it means a much shorter poem.

Ask other members of your group to look at both poems and say which one they prefer.

ACTIVITY

3 ACTIVITY

You could have some fun modelling the following poem by Adrian Henri.

Try about ten 'without you' fantasies. Searching for the unusual, the colourful, even the bizarre and disarming statement, is an excellent exercise to help develop your creative ability.

Points to model:
- obviously, the 'without you . . .' pattern
- the very clever mix of the simple little pleasures of life: 'they'd forget to put the salt in every packet of crisps'
- the simple yet ingenious thought: 'it would be an offence punishable by a fine of up to £200 or two months imprisonment to be found in possession of curry powder'
- and the truly bizarre: 'I'd spend my summers picking morosely over the remains of train crashes'.

Without You

Without you every morning would be like going back to work after a holiday,
Without you I couldn't stand the smell of the East Lancs Road,
Without you ghost ferries would cross the Mersey manned by skeleton crews,
Without you I'd probably feel happy and have more money and time and nothing to do with it,
Without you I'd have to leave my stillborn poems on other people's doorsteps, wrapped in brown paper,
Without you there'd never be sauce to put on sausage butties,
Without you plastic flowers in shop windows would just be plastic flowers in shop windows
Without you I'd spend my summers picking morosely over the remains of train crashes,
Without you white birds would wrench themselves free from my paintings and fly off dripping blood into the night,
Without you green apples wouldn't taste greener,
Without you Mothers wouldn't let their children play out after tea,
Without you every musician in the world would forget how to play the blues,
Without you Public Houses would be public again,
Without you the Sunday Times colour supplement would come out in black-and-white,
Without you indifferent colonels would shrug their shoulders and press the button,
Without you they'd stop changing the flowers in Piccadilly Gardens,
Without you Clark Kent would forget how to become Superman,
Without you Sunshine Breakfast would only consist of Cornflakes,
Without you there'd be no colour in Magic colouring books
Without you Mahler's 8th would only be performed by street musicians in derelict houses,
Without you they'd forget to put the salt in every packet of crisps,
Without you it would be an offence punishable by a fine of up to £200 or two months imprisonment to be found in possession of curry powder,
Without you riot police are massing in quiet sidestreets,

Without you all streets would be one-way the other way,
Without you there'd be no one not to kiss goodnight when we quarrel,
Without you the first martian to land would turn round and go away again,
Without you they'd forget to change the weather,
Without you blind men would sell unlucky heather,
Without you there would be
no landscapes/no stations/no houses,
no chipshops/no quiet villages/no seagulls
on beaches/no hopscotch on pavements/no
night/no morning/there'd be no city no country
Without you.

ADRIAN HENRI

Irony

Use the following poem as a model for your own ironic poem—one which uses words in a mockingly humourous way, where the intended meaning is the *opposite* of what is actually said. *On the Seventh Day* is modelled on the opening verses of the Old Testament of the Bible.

Points to model:
- the beginning phrase: 'in the end'; try a variation perhaps
- the similar, sequential beginnings of subsequent verses
- the frequent use of 'and' and the free-flowing rhythm (virtually no punctuation) which produce an effect of feverish, thoughtless activity
- the frequent repetition of 'And Man' (with a capital letter, note), and the final, repeated line of most verses 'And Man said, "It is good"', to create a similar and ironic tone of brash, unthinking confidence in so-called 'progress' and development
- the final irony of the closing lines.

Try to introduce some pattern or 'craft' in your poem; in other words, make sure it doesn't degenerate into pure prose style.

On The Seventh Day

In the end,
There was Earth, and it was of form and beauty.
And Man dwelt upon the lands of the Earth, the
meadows and trees, and he said,
'Let us build our dwellings in this place of beauty'
And he built cities and covered the earth with concrete
    and steel
And the meadows were gone,
And Man said, 'It is good'.

On the second day, Man looked upon the waters of the
    Earth.
And Man said, 'Let us put our wastes in the waters so
    that the dirt will be washed away'.
And Man did.
And the waters became polluted and foul in smell.
And Man said, 'It is good'.

On the third day, Man looked upon the forests of the
    Earth and saw they were beautiful.

And Man said, 'Let us cut the timber for our homes
   and grind the wood for our use'.
And the lands became barren and the trees were gone.
And man said, 'It is good'.

On the fourth day, Man saw that animals were in abundance
   and ran in the fields and played in the sun.
And Man said, 'Let us chase these animals for our amusement
   and kill them for our sport.'
And Man did.
And there were no more animals on the face of the Earth.
And Man said, 'It is good.'

On the fifth day, Man breathed the air of the Earth,
And Man said, 'Let us dispose of our wastes into the
   air, for the winds shall blow them away'.
And Man did.
And the air became heavy with dust and all living
   things burned and choked.

On the sixth day, Man saw himself, and saw the many
   languages and tongues he feared and hated.
And Man said, 'Let us build great machines and destroy
   these lest they destroy us'.
And Man built great machines and the Earth was fired
   with the rage of wars.
And Man said, 'It is good'.

On the seventh day, Man rested from his labours and the
   Earth was still, for Man no longer dwelt upon the Earth.
AND IT WAS GOOD.

(SOURCE UNKNOWN)

5
ACTIVITY

Satire

With very little change to a traditional nursery rhyme you can create a
brief but hard-hitting satire of an aspect of our modern world. Use the
following examples to model your own satirical poems.

Hey Diddle Diddle

Hey diddle diddle
The physicists fiddle,
   The bleep jumped over the moon.
The little dog laughed to see such fun
   And died the following June.

PAUL DEHN

Little Miss Muffet

   Little Miss Muffet
   Crouched on a tuffet,
Collecting her shell-shocked wits.
   There dropped from a glider
   An H-bomb beside her—
Which frightened Miss Muffet to bits.

PAUL DEHN

6
ACTIVITY

The following poem by Bruce Dawe is very cleverly based on its
Biblical original and satirizes a tedious aspect of our working world.
Before reading it, check the meanings of: magenta, conundrums, ar-
ticulation, barbiturate, liturgy and inexorable.

Choose a topic that you find worthy of satire—something tedious, repetitive or unjust perhaps—and use *Beatitudes* as your model for a satirical poem.

Points to model:
- the 'Blessed' introduction to each line or comment (try about six such patterns)
- the lengthy list that concludes the poem and reinforces the feeling of interminable monotony
- the use of imagery: 'the barbiturate of years', 'the desk calendar's inexorable snow', 'the punch-card fantasies', 'the complete liturgy of longing'.

Beatitudes

Blessed are the files marked ACTION in the INWARD tray,
    for they shall be actioned;
Blessed are the memos from above stamped forthrightly
    in magenta FOR IMMEDIATE ATTENTION,
        for they shall receive it;
Blessed are the telephones that chirrup and the marvellous
    conundrums conveyed thereby;
Blessed also the intercom calling this one or that from
    his labours that he may enter into the Presence;
Blessed the air-conditioning system bringing a single guaranteed
    hygienic weather within these walls;
Blessed the discreet articulation of management
    by whose leave the heart beats;
Blessed the barbiturate of years, the desk-calendar's
    inexorable snow, the farewells rippling the typing-pool's
        serenity, the Christmas Eve parties where men choke quietly
            over the unaccustomed cigar and the elderly file-clerks
                squeal at the shy randyness of their seniors;
Blessed the punch-card fantasies of the neat young men
    whom only the blotter's doodling betrays;
Blessed the complete liturgy of longing, the stubbed grief,
    the gulped joy, the straightened seams, the Glo-weave yes,
        the rubberized love, the shined air, the insensible clouds,
            the dream rain and see there over and above
                the rainbow's wrecked girders
                    the pterodactyl smile . . .

BRUCE DAWE

Society, by Michael Dransfield, is a clever satire on the monotony and regularity of our everyday lives. You could use a similar form for a satire on a topic of your choosing—for example: a particular institution, event or tradition, such as school, jail, public transport, public examinations, Christmas shopping, daily rituals, etc.

Or, like Dransfield, you could deal with society in general.

Points to model:
- the simple series of statements (try at least six of your own)

7
ACTIVITY

- the very flat *tone* achieved by concise, factual statement; no description, elaboration or direct comment, just a matter-of-fact account of what is happening
- the careful selection of official-sounding words: 'categories, compartments, official function, authorized, specified', etc; some repeated for further impact
- the particular impact of the final statement: 'nothing will occur'. See if you can create an impact with your final line.

Society

1. The citizens group in categories/officials, wives, children, priests, revolutionaries.

2. They enter the compartment assigned to their category/classroom, office, kitchen, garret.

3. The compartments are then sealed/from within/by the official whose function is to seal.

4. Each compartment has been scientifically designed/nothing is wasted/each contains
    (a) equipment necessary to its correct functioning;
    (b) for decoration, one item of official art; and
    (c) a window with an authorised view, designed to be pleasant.

5. The citizens perform their duties/as required/as trained/as usual.

6. At specified intervals, the citizens may stop work/look out the window/at the view. Refreshment is dispensed/from a machine/tea from one tap, coffee from another/sugar, milk/all is hygienic.

7. Citizens resume their duties.

8. When their time-quota is completed, citizens file out, regroup, return to home cubicles/transport is provided.

9. On arriving home, citizens will change from duty wear to recreational uniform.

10. Citizens will perform the functions of eating, cleaning body & uniform, resting, engaging in specified social activities.

11. After a specified interval, citizens
will regroup in categories/regroup the
day is sealed from within/nothing is
wasted/nothing will occur.

MICHAEL DRANSFIELD

Feeling

Read Walt Whitman, below, in a very pensive and critical mood. Now,
list all the wrongs and heartache that *you* see in the world, and write
them up in a similar style.

Alternatively, you may like to follow a similar pattern but write of
what is good and admirable about humanity and the world, adopting a
lighter tone and rhythm. In either case, let your deeper feelings come
through.

Points to model:
- each critical statement starting with 'I'
- the 'I' sometimes repeated within a line to give a heavy, rhythmic
  balance
- frequent punctuated listing (for example, line 6), again adding to the
  heavy, oppressive rhythm and tone.
- final, gripping lines that sum up the poem 'All these . . .', 'See, hear,
  and am silent'.

I sit and look out upon all the sorrows of the world, and upon
   all oppression and shame,
I hear secret convulsive sobs from the young men at anguish with
   themselves, remorseful after deeds done,
I see in low life the mother misused by her children, dying,
   neglected, gaunt, desperate,
I see the wife misused by her husband, I see the treacherous
   seducer of young women,
I mark the ranklings of jealously and unrequited love attempted
   to be hid, I see these sights on earth,
I see the workings of battle, pestilence, tyranny, I see martyrs
   and prisoners,
I observe famine at sea, I observe sailors casting lots who
   shall be killed to preserve the lives of the rest,
I observe the slights and degradations cast by arrogant persons
   upon laborers, the poor, and upon Negroes, and the like;
All these—all the meanness and agony without end I sitting
   look out upon,
See, hear, and am silent.

WALT WHITMAN

Form

ACTIVITY

Now try your hand at modelling specific poetic forms. You can refer back to those you investigated in chapter 5 (pages 71-73) for further help—and inspiration.

Sonnet

from *Sonnets From The Portuguese*

How do I love thee? Let me count the ways.
  I love thee to the depth and breadth and height
  My soul can reach, when feeling out of sight
For the ends of Being and ideal Grace.
I love thee to the level of every day's
  Most quiet need, by sun and candlelight.
  I love thee freely, as men strive for Right;
I love thee purely, as they turn from Praise.
I love thee with the passions put to use
  In my old griefs, and with my childhood's faith.
I love thee with a love I seemed to lose
  With my lost saints,—I love thee with the breath,
Smiles, tears, of all my life!—and, if God choose,
  I shall but love thee better after death.

ELIZABETH BARRETT BROWNING

Lyric

In The Bush

I follow the path into the bush
Until I reach a creek,
Deep in the forest.

I sit on a log,
Look up,
And can hardly see the sky.

This is my first time in the bush.
I wonder
and wonder.
I tell myself
I can conquer
Fear and wilderness.

I would rather be somewhere else
For here I feel wary.
Yet . . .
The taste of the air takes me to the top.

I realise how good it is,
The enjoyment,
The birdsong,
Singing rhythm.

QUOC AN HUA
(STUDENT)

Remember

Remember me when I am gone away,
Gone far away into the silent land;
When you can no more hold me by the hand,
Nor I half turn to go, yet turning stay.
Remember me when no more, day by day,
You tell me of our future that you planned;
Only remember me; you understand
It will be late to counsel then or pray.
Yet if you should forget me for a while
And afterwards remember, do not grieve;
For if the darkness and corruption leave
A vestige of the thoughts that once I had,
Better by far you should forget and smile
Than that you should remember and be sad.

CHRISTINA ROSSETTI

Blank verse

Reported Missing

Can you give me a precise description?
Said the policeman. Her lips, I told him,
Were soft. Could you give me, he said, pencil
Raised, a metaphor? Soft as an open mouth,
I said. Were there any noticeable
Peculiarities? he asked. Her hair hung
Heavily, I said. Any particular
Colour? he said. I told him I could recall
Little but its distinctive scent. What do
You mean, he asked, by distinctive? It had
The smell of woman's hair, I said. Where
Were you? he asked. Closer than I am to
Anyone at present, I said, level
With her mouth, level with her eyes. Her eyes?
He said, what about her eyes? There were two,
I said, both black. It has been established,
He said, that eyes cannot, outside common
Usage, be black; are you implying that
Violence was used? Only the gentle
Hammer blow of her kisses, the scent
Of her breath, the . . . Quite, said the policeman,
Standing, but I regret that we know of
No one answering to that description.

BARRY COLE

8

Inspirations

*I*n this final chapter you will take your own poetry composition one step further, writing in response to various written and visual stimuli. You will see, too, that some of the greatest sources of inspiration are your own life experiences and the world around you.

Two of the activities which follow—'Re-shaping the news' and 'Brainstorming'—are designed to be worked in groups.

Re-shaping the news

ACTIVITY 1

This is a challenging task for a small group of collaborative 'newspaper editors'.

1 Gather newspapers and collect headlines that you feel could be used as lines (or part lines) in a poem. You can gather these randomly or with some *thematic* purpose—for example, you may want your poem to make a statement about one of the following topics:
  • international relations
  • politics—local, state or federal
  • crime
  • business, investment
  • tragedy, accidents or tragic accidents
  • advertising—captions and slogans would be appropriate
  • industrial news, strikes or employment
  • human interest stories and events
  • fact and opinion—eg letters to the editor

- social events or news
- a specific topic or issue, eg conservation
- movie or TV ads and attractions.

This list is certainly not exhaustive; you may come up with other ideas. Alternatively, you may wish to choose headlines from a combination of categories.

2 As a group, juggle your headlines and add comments or lines of your own until you feel you have made your statement in a reasonably poetic way.

Remember: 'the best words in their best order' for maximum impact.

Metaphor and personification

ACTIVITY

The following brief poems are each based on one clever and extended metaphor. Look around you. Can you find suitable metaphors to cleverly describe and/or satirize some of the 'trappings' of your world?

An Edible Woman

Cake woman
first you were just a child,
just a bowl of sweet things,
waiting to be made

Cake woman
Made by fair hands
Cooking slowly to a mature woman
then coated with the icing
of society, perfection

Cake woman
beginning to crumble
First being sliced by the knife
of a broken heart

Cake woman
destroyed by the sins
of jealousy, hatred,
gluttony and vice

Cake woman
just crumbs now
shattered by the world
eaten up by the hungry mouths
of the rat race

ALTHEA McKENZIE
(STUDENT)

Apartment House

A filing-cabinet of human lives
Where people swarm like bees in tunneled hives,
Each to his own cell in the towered comb,
Identical and cramped—we call it home.

GERALD RAFTERY

On Watching the Construction of a Skyscraper

Nothing sings from these orange trees,
Rindless steel as smooth as sapling skin,
Except a crane's brief wheeze
And all the muffled, clanking din
Of rivets nosing in like bees.

BURTON RAFFEL

3
ACTIVITY

These short poems are each based on a *personification* of their subject. In other words, the poets have seen the life-like actions or characteristics of their subjects and built their poems around this perception.

Again, look around you, and choose something that you could personify in a brief poem.

Steam Shovel

The dinosaurs are not all dead.
I saw one raise its iron head
To watch me walking down the road
Beyond our house today.
Its jaws were dripping with a load
Of earth and grass that it had cropped
It must have heard me where I stopped,
Snorted white steam my way,
And stretched its long neck out to see,
And chewed, and grinned quite amiably.

CHARLES MALAM

The Toaster

A silver-scaled Dragon with jaws flaming red
Sits at my elbow and toasts my bread.
I hand him fat slices, and then, one by one,
He hands them back when he sees they are done.

WILLIAM JAY SMITH

The Garden Hose

In the gray evening
I see a long green serpent
With its tail in the dahlias.

It lies in loops across the grass
And drinks softly at the faucet.

I can hear it swallow.

BEATRICE JANOSCO

Seeing the poetry around you

The key to the poems which follow is simplicity. They show the poet's capacity to see and appreciate detail, to look and listen closely; to see poetry in a simple setting, and, finally, they show the poet's capacity to present these images with form and feeling.

Look for a moment at Karen Johns' poem about an early morning journey.

Early Morning Bus Ride

Slicing through the waning darkness
Humanity huddled together
No merry greetings
No words to crack the silence
Like an ancient ritual
Night falls away
Dawn is the victor
The city, the prize.

KAREN JOHNS
(STUDENT)

In a mere 32 words she has created an image of what her journey into the city is like.

See if you can find five or six words that describe your early morning experiences of either getting up or going out.

4
ACTIVITY

When you have those words try to work them into the lines of a short poem as Karen Johns has done. You may be pleased or dissatisfied by what you have written. Pause for a moment and look at the poems that follow, each capturing a particular moment. When you have read them, choose a moment, a place, or a person of your own to capture on paper.

Late Winter

The pallid cuckoo
Sent up in frail
Microtones
His rising scale
On the cold air.
What joy I found
Mounting that tiny
Stair of sound.

JAMES McAULEY

Bondi Afternoon 1915

Elioth Gruner

The wind plays through
the painted weather.

No cloud. The sea
and air, one blue.

A hemisphere
away from gunfire
an artist finds
his image for the year:

a girl in white
blown muslin, walking

in the last
clear afternoon.

GEOFF PAGE

Ryokan

at the window
rain

the sparrow
feathers puffed out

sings brightly but alone

my hand makes
black marks on white

the sparrow
pink marks on grey

MICHAEL DRANSFIELD

Components

Here are
blue teapot,
aluminium air.

A yellow desk,
straw matting,
wheaten lines of dusk.

A mango tree,
light climbing down
from day.

And distant thunder
walking into glass.

Here are
three components
equally clear.

The sound
of a millet broom
on stony ground.

A child's fist
pounding on boards
without rest.

A woman's voice
warping the afternoon
with its one choice.

ROGER McDONALD

City Sunset (i)

On a freshly
lain blue sky
drips the brok
en yolk of sun
light.
Soon darkness
ambles on and
wipes
away the traces.

City Sunset (ii)

Tall buildings
poised
like chessmen
in cloudy fingers.
Sneaky old sun
makes
a last move.

City Sunrise

the smoke
stalks up,
licks the
raw red
underbelly
of morning.

Morning Breakfast

The
morning breaks
      an egg in the
      frying pan

while
curtains draw

      cornflakes
      in a bowl.

STEVE TURNER

In Suburbia

Early morning, a suburban dawn,
Sun beats down on a close-cut lawn.
Monday morning, the alarm clock rings,
You get out of bed and do it again.

The cat on the steps, a cold hungry stare,
Exactly the look some people wear.
Another day, and your world's not changed.
Everything is just the same—again.

She says, 'Say you love me'. So you say you do.
'I thought it didn't mean that much to you'.
Then pull off your head and toss it to the sky
While another politician lies—again.

Another four-year-old just spat in your eye.
There isn't any truth, there isn't any lie.
Just LIFE, a four-letter word
As the establishment dies—again.

The supermarket eats the corner store.
Now that it's started, it will just want more.
You say, 'There isn't anything left to destroy'.
It devours itself. What a useful ploy—again.

Truth becomes a different sort of lie.
The answers are all in the question, 'Why?'
They put on their uniforms and forget about existence
And do it all—again.

BARRY GYTE
(STUDENT)

Winter

The heavy mist is lifted from the river bed,
Disclosing cattle, grouped forlornly in the cold.
They move slowly onto the flat to catch
The first glimmer of a shy sun.
As they move, they disturb the brittle
Frost-coated grass of the winter pasture,
Showering shards of glass between their cloven
                              hooves.

In the hut, the stockmen rise.
Uttering muffled curses and shaking with the cold
They make their way to start the fire.
Their numb fingers fumble with the matches that
                    snap too easily.
They hasten to gather around the flame that warms
                    them.

Their dogs are outside, huddled under the tractor.
Curled in a ball, they whimper gently,
Waiting for the fickle sunlight to reach them.

Winter has arrived.

LYNNE TEICHMANN
(STUDENT)

Brainstorming

You can approach this activity in small groups (each with a scribe) or as a whole class (with the teacher as blackboard scribe). Your task is to respond freely and spontaneously to each (one at a time) of the poems and visual images that follow.

The word 'brainstorming' means just that—sudden ideas, bursts of thought or emotion; uncensored and not laboured over. In a brainstorming session all contributions of ideas, feelings and suggestions must be recorded: no comments on, or criticisms of, contributions are allowed in the first stage.

1 Brainstorm your initial responses for about three minutes, the scribe recording everything.

2 The scribe then follows suggestions for deleting potentially irrelevant contributions. Don't be too hasty in this; sometimes an unlikely comment can become a truly creative one in the right context.

3 Now the scribe takes on the role of editor and chooses a first line for the poem from one of the ideas on the board. The idea may be modified or extended if desired.

4 The second and subsequent lines are chosen in the same way, with everyone contributing ideas and suggestions until all have been exhausted. Don't worry too much at this stage about the finer points of form, rhyme and rhythm—just focus on the content.

5 Erase all but this 'first draft'. Now concentrate on the finer points of your 'poem' until you are convinced that you have 'the best words in their best order'.

Note

The poems, photographs and advertisements that follow are for your reading and to help your ideas but they are not intended as models.

Concentrate mainly on whatever idea, message or picture you have.

Summary

In brief, brainstorming involves
• rapid writing
• editing
• finding a first line
• adding, line by line
• improving the poem

A Green Sportscar

. . . And later, to come across
those couples in gleaming green sportscars
riveted with steel and sprinkled with dawn;
and still shaking in tarpaulin hoods, the rain
spills onto their faces
as the daylight exposes their E-type deaths.

. . . And later still, to discover
inside him, something has been moved.
She stretched out across him, breasts
pointing towards dawn, who found her last kick
in the sound of the skid on tarmac
of the green-steel-coffin in its quiet field.

. . . And finally, to understand them;
they who having been switched off permanently,
are so very still. You would think them asleep,
not dead, if not for the evidence, their expressions
caught at dawn, and held tight beneath
this accidental incident.

BRIAN PATTEN

Ballad of Faith

No dignity without chromium
No truth but a glossy finish
If she purrs she's virtuous
If she hits ninety she's pure

ZZZZZZZZZ!
Step on the gas, brother
(the horn sounds hoarsely)

WILLIAM CARLOS WILLIAMS

Jigsaws

Property! Property! Let us extend
Soul and body without end:
A box to live in, with airs and graces
A box on wheels that shows its paces,
A box that talks or that makes faces,
And curtains and fences as good as the neighbours
To keep out the neighbours and keep us immured
Enjoying the cold canned fruit of our labours
In a sterilized cell, unshared, insured.

LOUIS MACNEICE

STADHAMPTON £120,000 –
Detached chalet in quiet lane
overlooking fields & farmland
beyond.

MORTON VILLAGE
£225,000 – Superb 3/4 bed
detached bungalow. 3/4
receps, gas ch, garage,
gardens.

Houses

People who are afraid of themselves
multiply themselves into families
and so divide themselves
and so become less afraid.

People who might have to go out
into clanging strangers' laughter,
crowd under roofs, make compacts
to no more than smile at each other.

People who might meet their own faces
or surprise their own faces in doorways,
build themselves rooms without mirrors
and live between walls without echoes.

People who might meet other faces
and unknown voices round corners
build themselves rooms all mirrors
and live between walls all echoes.

People who are afraid to go naked
clothe themselves in families, houses,
but are still afraid of death
because death one day will undress them.

A. S. J. TESSIMOND

EVERLEY

CHARMING well renovated 3
storey brick Cottage with 2 double
bedrooms, gas CH, fitted kitchen.
Good order throughout and long
rear garden.
£74,950

DIVINITY ROAD £135,000 – 3
bed det with 3 rec. Well restored,
with gas ch & gardens.

OLD ROAD £192,000 – Luxurious
new detached house built to a very
high specification.

from *Essay on Man*

Know then thyself, presume not God to scan;
The proper study of mankind is Man.
Placed on this isthmus of a middle state,
A being darkly wise, and rudely great:
With too much knowledge for the sceptic side,
With too much weakness for the stoic's pride,
He hangs between; in doubt to act, or rest,
In doubt to deem himself a god, or beast;
In doubt his mind or body to prefer,
Born but to die, and reasoning but to err;
Alike in ignorance, his reason such,
Whether he thinks too little, or too much:
Chaos of thought and passion, all confused;
Still by himself abused, or disabused;
Created half to rise, and half to fall;
Great lord of all things, yet a prey to all;
Sole judge of truth, in endless error hurled:
The glory, jest, and riddle of the world!

ALEXANDER POPE

from *As you Like It*
(Act II Scene VII)

All the world's a stage,
And all the men and women merely players:
They have their exits and their entrances;
And one man in his time plays many parts,
His acts being several ages. At first the infant,
Mewling and puking in the nurse's arms,
And then the whining school-boy, with his satchel
And shining morning face, creeping like snail
Unwillingly to school. And then the lover,
Sighing like a furnace, with a woeful ballad
Made to his mistress' eyebrow. Then a soldier,
Full of strange oaths and bearded like the pard,
Jealous in honour, sudden and quick in quarrel,
Seeking the bubble reputation
Even in the cannon's mouth. And then the justice,
In fair round belly with good capon lined,
With eyes severe and beard of formal cut,
Full of wise saws and modern instances
And so he plays his part. The sixth age shifts
Into the lean and slipper'd pantaloon,
With spectacles on nose and pouch on side,
His youthful hose, well saved, a world too wide
For his shrunk shank; and his big manly voice,
Turning again toward childish treble, pipes
And whistles in his sound. Last scene of all,
That ends this strange eventful history,
Is second childishness and mere oblivion,
Sans teeth, sans eyes, sans taste, sans every thing.

WILLIAM SHAKESPEARE

Those Other Times

There is a lack of austerity now
which makes me wonder
about the time
when people crowded railway stations
meeting trains
loaded to the hilt
with boys
shot-full of war.

How many women
took away from stations
memories of how chestnut
was his hair,
the smell and softness of his flesh
beneath khaki of army drill.
Now he is a name in copper plaque
weeping its green brass
into parks.

And the women went to one-room flats
and struggled with a child,
gift of war
the night the rumour went around
that leave was up.
Or single, to that new address,
the 'bed-sit'
which in its name defined
the post-war loveless years.

ROBYN ROWLAND

In True Life?

Behind veils
we enact our meaningless charades
that are our lives.

We shamble through
the stage show
of life,
inadequate actors
in an elaborate set.

We gain
mock friendships
through false pretence,
meaningless fame
through feigned bravado.

In blind frustration
we attempt to wrest
the masks
off fellow players
and bare them
to the ridicule
of the critics.

But

Often in the attempt
our own veils
are rent,
displaying us
to those who dare
see
the realism of mortality.

IAN PIEPER
(STUDENT)

Stimulations

Respond as an individual to any of the following stimuli. Although you are working alone, you may find it useful to follow the steps outlined in 'Brainstorming' on pages 125–126.

As well, you can provide your own 'stimulations'—poems, paintings or other visual images which appeal to you or bring up a response in you.

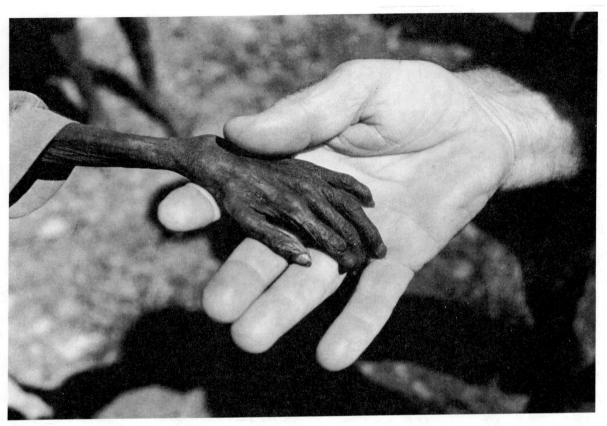

LIFE Magazine photographer Mike Wells, of the United States, won the World Press Photo 1980 award for this picture captioned 'Drought's Harvest in Uganda.'

Vampire, by Edvard Munch
(1863–1944)

The night is darkening round me,
The wild winds coldly blow;
But a tyrant spell has bound me
And I cannot, cannot go.

The giant trees are bending
Their bare boughs weighed with snow,
And the storm is fast descending
And yet I cannot go.

Clouds beyond clouds above me,
Wastes beyond wastes below;
But nothing drear can move me;
I will not, cannot go.

EMILY JANE BRONTE

Faces in the Street

They lie, the men who tell us, for reasons of their own,
That want is here a stranger, and that misery's unknown;
For where the nearest suburb and the city proper meet
My window-sill is level with the faces in the street—
      Drifting past, drifting past,
      To the beat of weary feet—
While I sorrow for the owners of those faces in the street.

And cause I have to sorrow, in a land so young and fair,
To see upon those faces stamped the marks of Want and Care;
I look in vain for traces of the fresh and fair and sweet
In sallow, sunken faces that are drifting through the street—
      Drifting on, drifting on,
      To the scrape of restless feet;
I can sorrow for the owners of the faces in the street.

In hours before the dawning dims the starlight in the sky
The wan and weary faces first begin to trickle by,
Increasing as the moments hurry on with morning feet,
Till like a pallid river flow the faces on the street—
      Flowing in, flowing in,
      To the beat of hurried feet—
Ah! I sorrow for the owners of those faces in the street.

The human river dwindles when 'tis past the hour of eight,
Its waves go flowing faster in the fear of being late;
But slowly drag the moments, whilst beneath the dust and heat,
The city grinds the owners of the faces in the street—
      Grinding body, grinding soul,
      Yielding scarce enough to eat—
Oh! I sorrow for the owners of the faces in the street.

And then the only faces till the sun is sinking down
Are those of outside toilers and the idlers of the town,
Save here and there a face that seems a stranger in the street,
Tells of the city's unemployed upon their weary beat—
      Drifting round, drifting round,
      To the tread of listless feet—
Ah! my heart aches for the owner of that sad face in the street.

And when the hours on lagging feet have slowly dragged away,
And sickly yellow gaslights rise to mock the going day,
Then, flowing past my window, like a tide in its retreat,
Again I see the pallid stream of faces in the street—
      Ebbing out, ebbing out,
      To the drag of tired feet,
While my heart is aching dumbly for the faces in the street.

HENRY LAWSON

Nietzche's Monstrance by R.B. Kitaj (b.1923)

To Sonny

Let's ride away, you and I,
On a horse as wild as our souls;
From cities and crowds and company strife,
Pressing in to mould us into their form,
Taking over our souls and bending our minds.
Let's ride to a valley surrounded by
   mountains,
Where horses run wild, and people are free;
Let the world of big business, where society
   rules,
Spin out of control without us.

JENNIFER FRY
(STUDENT)

The Scream by Edvard Munch (1863–1944)

1,000,000 Minutes of Peace

A non-denominational, non-political campaign for the United Nations International Year of Peace

Peace. In just a few minutes.

A Minute of Positive Thoughts

To think of peace for just one minute is like holding the world in your hands and seeing it as a whole. As one human family.

To have positive thoughts of peace is to appreciate all the work that is being done to make the world an easier place to live.

To be positive about peace is to understand that although I may not be able to stop war or terrorism, I can change my own thoughts and feelings—as I see that peace also begins with me.

To think positively about peace is to fill my attitude and actions with peace and share that with others.

With our combined positive thoughts of peace we can then actively work together towards a united peaceful world.

A Minute of Meditation

Sitting in a comfortable position I turn my attention inwards.

I am aware of many thoughts moving through my mind.

The speed of my thoughts begins to slow.

I focus my attention on a star of radiant light within my mind, and I create quiet thoughts of peace.

Slowly my mind becomes like the surface of a lake, completely calm, totally still.

I experience a deep silence as I become aware that I am peace.

And I spread the power of that light, of that peace, across the world.

A Minute of Prayer

God make me an Instrument of Your peace;
where there is hatred, let me sow love;
where there is injury, pardon;
where there is doubt, faith;
where there is despair, hope;
where there is darkness, light;
and where there is sadness, joy.

That I may seek to console rather than to be consoled,
to understand rather than to be understood, to love
rather than to be loved.

For it is in giving that we receive;
in self-forgetfulness that we find our true selves,
in forgiving that we are forgiven,
in dying that we are raised up to
life everlasting.

God, make me an instrument of Your peace.

ST. FRANCIS OF ASSISI

A Minute of Inspiration

Write your own message of peace to the world.

Word play

Some poets are delightfully creative, using words in refreshingly new ways and patterns. These poems are examples of such clever word play.

After Some Thought, A Poem

if i grow a
moustache
for you
will you grow a
ffectionate
for me?

STEVE TURNER

In and Out of Joyce's Daydream

One and one is two,
Two and two is four,
Three and three are the times I
watched the weakness in your wandering eye waver
as lovers for the first times two kissed, without a
care.
Two times two is four,
Three times three is the smoothness of
your skin is so sublime times nine is seventy-two days
now you have gone. I wanted to tell you how I, don't
   know the answer,
miss your loving gaze.
I stare at your empty seat.

'James! 12 times 11 is 132.'
'Yes miss' you.

DARREN BOWGET
(STUDENT)

i thank You God for most this amazing
day: for the leaping greenly spirits of trees
and a blue true dream of sky; and for everything
which is natural which is infinite which is yes

(i who have died am alive again today,
and this is the sun's birthday; this is the birth
day of life and of love and wings: and of the gay
great happening illimitably earth)

how should tasting touching hearing seeing
breathing any—lifted from the no
of all nothing—human merely being
doubt unimaginable You?

(now the ears of my ears awake and
now the eyes of my eyes are opened)

e. e. cummings

Fern Hill

Now as I was young and easy under the apple boughs
About the lilting house and happy as the grass was green,
    The night above the dingle starry,
      Time let me hail and climb
    Golden in the heydays of his eyes,
And honoured among wagons I was prince of the apple towns
And once below a time I lordly had the trees and leaves
      Trail with daisies and barley
    Down the rivers of the windfall light.

And as I was green and carefree, famous among the barns
About the happy yard and singing as the farm was home,
    In the sun that is young once only,
      Time let me play and be
    Golden in the mercy of his means,
And green and golden I was huntsman and herdsman, the calves
Sang to my horn, the foxes on the hills barked clear and cold,
      And the sabbath rang slowly
    In the pebbles of the holy streams.

All the sun long it was running, it was lovely, the hay
Fields high as the house, the tunes from the chimneys, it was air
    And playing, lovely and watery
      And fire green as grass.
    And nightly under the simple stars
As I rode to sleep the owls were bearing the farm away,
All the moon long I heard, blessed among stables, the nightjars
    Flying with the ricks, and the horses
      Flashing into the dark.

And then to awake, and the farm, like a wanderer white
With the dew, come back, the cock on his shoulder: it was all
    Shining, it was Adam and maiden,
      The sky gathered again
    And the sun grew round that very day.
So it must have been after the birth of the simple light
In the first, spinning place, the spellbound horses walking warm
    Out of the whinnying green stable
      On to the fields of praise.

And honoured among foxes and pheasants by the gay house
Under the new made clouds and happy as the heart was long,
    In the sun born over and over,
      I ran my heedless ways,
    My wishes raced through the house high hay
And nothing I cared, at my sky blue trades, that time allows
In all his tuneful turning so few and such morning songs
    Before the children green and golden
      Follow him out of grace,

Nothing I cared, in the lamb white days, that time would take me
Up to the swallow thronged loft by the shadow of my hand,
    In the moon that is always rising,
      Nor that riding to sleep
    I should hear him fly with the high fields

And wake to the farm forever fled from the childless land.
Oh as I was young and easy in the mercy of his means,
    Time held me green and dying
  Though I sang in my chains like the sea.

DYLAN THOMAS

One Summer

One summer you
aeroplaned away,
too much money
away for me, and
stayed there for
quite a few
missed embraces.

Before leaving,
you smiled me that
you'd return all of
a mystery moment and
would airletter me
every few breakfasts
in the meantime.
           This
you did, and I thank
you most kissingly.
             I
wish however, that I
could hijackerplane
to the Ignited States
of Neon where I'd
crash land perfectly
in the deserted
airport of your heart.

STEVE TURNER

A closer analysis of the poems reveals the following creative techniques:

1 **Unusual use of verbs:** 'I rode to sleep'.

2 **Creation of 'new' verbs:** 'aeroplaned away', 'airletter me'.

3 **Unusual use of adjectives:** 'as I was young and easy', 'about the lilting house', 'the children green and golden'.

4 **Unusual comparisons:** 'as happy as the grass was green'.

5 **Unusual personification:** 'My wishes raced through the house high hay'.

6 **Additions to common phrases:** 'in the first, spinning place', 'blue true dream of sky', 'human merely being'.

7 **Altered clichés:** 'once below a time', 'clear and cold', 'all the sun long', 'all of a mystery moment', 'every few breakfasts'.

8 **Concentrated juxtaposition of verbs, adverbs, adjectives:** 'the gay great happening illimitably earth'.

9 **Stream of consciousness fantasies**—where one idea cleverly leads to another: see *In and Out of Joyce's Daydream*.

10 **Clever word play:** see *After Some Thought, A Poem*.

The clever use of words is much more difficult than it seems but you might like to take a very ordinary object such as a garden or a bus stop and describe it in a new and unusual way.

7

ACTIVITY

Experiencing poetry

All of us, at some time or another, have had experiences that were beautiful, dramatic, tragic or moving; some of these could properly be called 'poetic' experiences, or 'the stuff of which poetry is made'. Sadly though, these experiences are usually never recorded, never captured in words and, so, forgotten. W.N. Scott in his wonderfully inspirational poem talks of this dilemma and recaptures the 'poetry' that has, to date, remained unpenned.

Hearing Yevtushenko, March 1966

All my best poems were never written down,
they sing in my skull and will not let me sleep.
They do not move as marks across white paper.

Once in grey weather, howling out of hell
in the aseptic south, we raised a lifeboat
over the rim of sea, and in it, locked in ice
three dead men. One had wrapped his coat
around his friend, who froze nevertheless
but took a minute longer in his dying
because of love and comradeship. That is a poem.

Once in the desert, at the copper mines
I helped to bury one who fell and died
eight hundred screaming feet to jagged rock.
We drank cold beer to his memory, then forgot him,
laughing like brazen bells under a sky
molten copper over hills of slag. That was a poem.

Once at a wedding among brown-skinned people
saw how the bridgegroom's eyes embraced his bride
and could not tell them how I loved them both,
could only smile, and nod, and hold my peace
not comprehending the rich jokes of my companions.

Then, in that great gilded theatre
one of a turmoil of dim oval faces
heard a young man accusing in his anger
the cruelty of man to man, and knew
that brotherhood is good, compassion good,

bravery and laughter, love and birth are good
and language is no wall when eyes can meet.
How lies and hatred vanish when two men
clasp hands in friendship with no other link
than hate of evil things and cruel things.

All my best poems were never written down
but courage drives the fear from my throat
to know another man has felt the same
and put our words to march in solemn order
across white paper. That is a poem, too.

W. N. SCOTT

8 ACTIVITY

Read Scott's poem carefully; appreciate its tone, feeling and imagery. Then think long and hard about any of your life experiences that could 'move as marks across white paper'. Of course, they may not seem as dramatic as this poet's experiences, but they'll exist nevertheless. Start your poem, too, with the line:

'All my best poems were never written down'.

Be prepared for a lot of trial, error and editing before you have a finished poem.

9 ACTIVITY

Opening lines

The following are all opening lines of published poems. They have been chosen because they are evocative and, sometimes, emotive; at least one of them may inspire you to write further. Choose one to be the first line of *your* poem.

All day, day after day, they're bringing them home
And indeed I shall anchor, one day—some summer morning
But
False dreams, all false
From troubles of the world
My sisters played beyond the doorway
Remember me when I am gone away
Tenderly, gently, the soft rain
When I am dead, my dearest
All human things are subject to decay
At the street corner, hunched up
At night, by the fire
Frau Antonia is a cabbage
As I walked out one evening
An old man whose black face
For us, born into a world
He thrust his joy against the weight of the sea
An afternoon late summer, in a room
Child looked up and saw
She walks in beauty, like the night

First the B52s
Monday to Friday, at the plant
When I awoke this morning
Why are you troubled, young man, young man?
I wander through each chartered street
When I am old and grey and full of sleep
Let us go then, you and I
Softly, at dusk, a woman is singing to me
The young dead soldiers do not speak
We are the hollow men
Who is Silvia? what is she?

Titles of poems in 'Instant reactions'

Poem beginning 'Retired a year now, Bert makes', page 4
Title: *Bert*

Poem beginning 'My mistress' eyes are nothing like the sun', page 6
Title: *My Mistress' Eyes are Nothing Like the Sun*

Poem beginning 'In the east', page 4
Title: *Twenty-Four Hour Forecast*

Poem beginning 'I heard them say I'm ugly.' page 5
Title: *The Ugly Child*

Poem beginning 'I heard a thousand blended notes', page 6
Title: *Lines Written in Early Spring*

Poem beginning 'I remember', page 7
Title: *First Love*

Acknowledgements

The author and the publishers would like to thank the following for permission to reproduce copyright material used in this book: Angus & Robertson Publishers for 'The Night Ride' and 'Beach Burial' by Kenneth Slessor from Now'; *Selected Poems*, © Paul Slessor, 1944; 'Evening' by Kevin Hart from *The Lines of the Hand*, © Kevin Hart, 1981; 'Cows' and 'City Cafeteria' by Peter Kocan from *Armistice*, © Peter Kocan, 1980; 'A Night of Rain', 'Served with Notice' and 'To a Friend Under Sentence of Death' by Anne Elder from *Crazy Women & Other Poems*, © Anne Elder, 1976; 'Election Speech' by Vincent Buckley from *Selected Poems*, © Vincent Buckley, 1981; 'Standardization' by A. D. Hope from *Collected Poems*, © A. D. Hope, 1966, 1969, 1972; 'Epitaph for a Monster of our Times' and 'At My Grandmother's' by David Malouf from *Selected Poems*, © David Malouf, 1981; 'The Commercial Hotel' by Les A. Murray from *The Vernacular Republic Poems 1961–81*, © Les A. Murray, 1982; 'Late Winter' by James McAuley from *Collected Poems 1936–70*, © Norma McAuley, 1971; 'Train Journey', 'The Company of Lovers', 'South of My Days' and 'Brothers and Sisters' by Judith Wright from *Collected Poems 1942–70*, © Judith Wright, 1971; *The Antioch Review* for 'On Watching the Construction of a Skyscraper' by Burton Raffel; The Australian National Gallery, Canberra for 'Child of the High Seas' by Joy Hester; Brahma Kumaris Raja Yoga Centre for 'Million Minutes of Peace'; Cadbury Ltd for 'In and Out of Joyce's Daydream' by Darrel Bowget; 'Logic', 'Peace of Mind', 'Atlantic Beach' and 'Borderline' by Rosemary Cowan; 'Love So Surprise' by Jan Harley; 'Skull' by Arnold Hunt'; 'Division' by Timothy Locker; 'Rose' by James Loxley; 'Requiem' by Pamela McKay; 'An Edible Woman' by Althea McKenzie; 'Yorkshire', 'The Boxer', 'Early Swim' and 'Dockland' by Emma Payne; 'My Friend's Head' by Katy Senior and 'A Prophecy' by Adam Stanley from *Cadbury's Third Book of Children's Poetry*, 1985; Ross Clark for 'Bert' and 'Tabula Rasa'; Jonathon Clowes for 'Reported Missing' by Barry Cole; Jeni Couzyn for 'The Door'; Paul Dehn for 'Hey Diddle Diddle' and 'Little Miss Muffet'; Francisco Campbell Custodio, Ad. Donker (Pty) Ltd for 'The Zulu Girl' by Roy Campbell; Faber & Faber Ltd for 'Jigsaws' and 'Prayer Before Birth' by Louis Macneice from *The Collected Poems of Louis Macneice*; 'Preludes' by T. S. Eliot from *Collected Poems 1909–1962*; and 'No Speech from the Scaffold' and 'Taylor Street' by Thom Gunn from *Touch*; Robert D. Fitzgerald for 'Deep Within Man'; Jennifer Fry for 'To Sonny'; Silvana Gardner for 'The Necklace'; Grafton Books for 'next to of course god america . . .', 'If there are any heavens . . .' and 'I thank You God for most this amazing' by e. e. cummings from *Complete Poems 1913–1962*; William Grono for 'The Way We Live Now'; Barry Gyte for 'In Suburbia'; R. G. Hay for 'Petition'; David Higham Associates Ltd for 'Do Not Go Gentle Into That Good Night', 'Fern Hill' and 'The Hunchbank in the Park' by Dylan Thomas from *The Poems*; Hodder & Stoughton Limited for 'City Sunrise', 'If Jesus was Born Today', 'In My World', 'Five Hundred Million Pounds', 'The Examination,' 'Daily London Recipe', 'The News and Weather', '7/8 of the Truth and Nothing But the Truth' 'City Sunset I', 'City Sunset II', 'Morning Breakfast', 'After Some Thought, A Poem' and 'One Summer' by Steve Turner from *Up to Date*; Henry Holt and Company, Inc. for 'Steam Shovel' by Charles Malam from *Upper Pasture*, © Charles Malam, 1930, 1958; Houghton Mifflin Company for 'The Young Dead Soldiers' by Archibald MacLeish from *New and Collected Poems 1917–1976*, © Archibald MacLeish; Flexmore Hudson for 'Drought'; Beatrice Janosco for 'The Garden Hose'; Karen Johns for 'Early Morning Bus Ride'; T. F. Kline for 'Emporium'; Longman Cheshire for 'Open Invitation' by Bruce Dawe from *Sometimes Gladness: Collected Poems 1954–1982*, 'In the New Landscape' and 'Beatitudes' by Bruce Dawe from *An Eye for a Tooth* and 'Drought' and 'Those Other Times' by Robyn Rowland from *Filigree In Blood*; Nicole Mathieson for 'Eulogy'; Melbourne University Press for 'The Searchers' by B. A. Breen; The National Gallery of Victoria for 'The Wire' by Noel Counihan and 'Dreaming in the Street' by Charles Blackman; A. D. Peters & Co Ltd for 'Sad Aunt Madge' by Roger McGough from *Modern Poets 10– The Mersey Sound*; Ian Pieper for 'In True Life'; Anita Pitcher for 'Why'; Queensland Newspapers for 'Forgotten Dreamtime' by Nadia Harmsen; 'First Love' by Elisabeth Mitchell; 'Maths vs Daydreaming' by Alison MacKenzie; 'The Achiever' by Susan Legget and 'Friendships' by Erica Fryberg, published in *Courier-Mail*, 1984–1986; and for the photographs on pages 127, 129, 130, 132, 133, 139; Quoc An Hua for 'In the Bush'; Gerald Raftery for 'Apartment House'; Craig Reed for 'Who Will Take Grandma?'; Deborah Rogers Ltd for 'Without You' by Adrian Henri; W. N. Scott for 'Hearing Yevtushenko'; Anthony Sheil Associates Ltd for 'Song For Last Year's Wife' and 'A Green Sportscar' by Brian Patten; Judy Shrimpton for 'I Followed a Butterfly'; William Jay Smith for 'The Toaster'; L. M. Teichman for 'Winter'; A. S. J. Tessimond for 'Houses'; United Press International for 'Drought's Harvest in Uganda' by Life Magazine photographer Mike Wells; University of Queensland Press for 'In the Forest' by Thomas Shapcott from *Selected Poems*, 1978; 'And No Birds Sing' by Michael Dransfield from *Voyage into Solitude*, 1978; 'Ryokan', 'Society' and 'Prosperity' by Michael Dransfield from *The Inspector of Tides*, 1972; 'Against or For Beauty' by Richard Tipping from *Domestic Hardcore*, 1975; 'Components' and 'Twenty-four Hour Forecast' by Roger McDonald from *Airship*, 1975; 'Bondi Afternoon, 1915' by Geoff Page from *Smalltown Memorial*, 1975; 'Church Grounds' by Robert Gray from *Creekwater Journal*, 1975; and 'Suburban Lullaby' by John Manifold from *Collected Verse*, 1978; William Carlos Williams for 'Ballad of Faith'. David Kitchen for 'Mr Smith's Collection'; J. D. Enright for 'Tourist Promotion' from *Collected Poems*, Oxford University Press; Penguin Books Ltd for 'A Boy's Head' from *Selected Poems* by Miroslav Holub, translated by Ian Milner and George Theiner (Penguin Modern European Poets, 1967,) © Miroslav Holub, 1967, translation copyright © Penguin Books 1967; Elizabeth Jennings for 'I heard them say I'm Ugly' from *Collected Poems*, Macmillan Publishers Ltd; Pat Arrowsmith for 'This Is Your Death'; William McIlvanney for 'Initiation' from *The Other Side of the Clyde*, ed. D. Drever, Puffin.

Every effort has been made to contact holders of copyright. However, the author and publisher would appreciate enquiries from any persons who believe they hold copyright to material used in this book.

The authors and publishers would like to thank the following for permission to reproduce photographs on the pages noted:
Robert Harding Picture Library, page 127 and page 128 left; J. Allen & Cash Ltd, page 129; Frank Spooner Pictures, page 132 top and bottom, page 132, page 139; Aspect Picture Library Limited, page 134; The Bridgeman Art Library and Christie's, London for *Umpire* by Edvard Munch, page 135; and Lord Gaurie Collection for *Nietzche's Monstrance* by Kitay, page 137; and National Gallery Oslo for *The Scream* by Edvard Munch, page 138.

Index to notes

Index of authors

Index of titles and first lines